ATTITUDES TO SCHOOL

of top primary and first-year secondary pupils

Wendy Keys
Sue Harris
Cres Fernandes

nfer

Published in November 1995
by the National Foundation for Educational Research,
The Mere, Upton Park, Slough, Berkshire SL1 2DQ

ISBN 0 7005 1400 7

CONTENTS

ACKNOWLEDGEMENTS

This study could not have been completed without the help of a large number of people and we would like to express our thanks to:

The students, teachers and headteachers in the schools which took part in the study;

Lesley Saunders, Dougal Hutchison and David Upton, who read and commented on the draft report;

Anne Milne and John Hanson in NFER's Field Research Services Department, who organised the administration of the study;

Mary Hargreaves who prepared the layout, Tim Wright, who designed the cover and Enver Carim, who coordinated the production of the report.

CHAPTER 1

INTRODUCTION

1.1   The background to the study

The study described in this report was carried out by the National Foundation for Educational Research in order to investigate an important issue identified in a previous project. This earlier research focused on the attitudes towards school of students in Year 7 and Year 9; these were reported in *What DO Students Think About School?* (Keys and Fernandes, 1993). A significant finding of this study was that by the end of their first year of secondary education, a minority of Year 7 pupils already held negative attitudes towards school (e.g. they did not like being at school, they found school work boring and thought that school was a waste of time). This finding raised an important question: had these pupils' negative attitudes been developed during their primary school years or since they had transferred to secondary school?

The study described in this report set out to investigate this question by comparing the attitudes towards school of pupils in their final year at primary school (Year 6) with pupils in their first year at secondary school (Year 7). Since the earlier study acted as the stimulus for the research described here, and since the views of first-year secondary pupils were surveyed in both studies, this document contains a number of references to the data from the earlier report. Whilst some readers will no doubt wish to read the report on the earlier study, others will find sufficient information relating to it summarised within this document. This report also highlights the differences between boys and girls in terms of their attitudes towards school and education – a topic not covered in the previous report – and compares the size of each gender difference found amongst top primary school children with the extent of the corresponding gender difference amongst first-year secondary school pupils.

1.2   The structure of the report

The following chapter (Chapter 2) describes the design of the study, the development and content of the questionnaires and gives details of the sampling and administration procedures. The next three chapters are concerned with the results of the analyses of pupils' responses to the questionnaire surveys: Chapter 3 compares the responses of the top primary and first-year secondary pupils to a range of questions concerning their experiences and behaviour in school and their attitudes towards school and education; Chapter 4 reports on specific gender differences; and Chapter 5 focuses on the responses of pupils who do not like school. Each of these chapters ends with a summary of the main findings. The final chapter (Chapter 6) provides an overview of the study and considers the main implications of the research. Background information on the pupils and schools taking part and details of the administration of the study are given in Appendices 1 and 2.

CHAPTER 2
THE DESIGN AND ADMINISTRATION OF THE STUDY

This chapter describes how the research was carried out and provides a summary of the main issues covered in the questionnaires for pupils and schools.

2.1 The design of the research

The main elements of the study were the questionnaire surveys of pupils in top primary (Year 6) and first-year secondary (Year 7) education. However, in order to ensure that the two samples of pupils were sufficiently homogeneous for the comparisons between the responses of pupils to be valid, the headteachers of each of the schools sampled were asked to complete a short questionnaire providing background information on the school.

The pupil questionnaire was adapted from the version used in the earlier study (Keys and Fernandes, 1993). Relatively few amendments were made so as to facilitate comparison between the responses of the first-year secondary pupils in each study, where appropriate. The questionnaire was substantially the same for both samples, although there were some changes in the text to reflect the fact that top primary pupils are normally taught by one (class) teacher whereas first-year secondary are usually taught by several teachers, for different subjects.

The questionnaire for top primary pupils was piloted on a sample of 54 pupils in three schools. As a result of the pilot, and accompanying comments from six teachers of these pupils, a number of questions received minor modifications.

During the administration of the survey, teachers were asked to emphasise two points to pupils. Firstly, since the questions asked for the pupils' opinions (i.e. there were no right and wrong answers), it was stressed that pupils should answer as honestly as they could. Secondly, the pupils' responses were treated as confidential: to reinforce the fact that neither the pupil's teacher(s), nor their headteacher, nor their parents would see their responses, pupils sealed their questionnaires in an envelope before handing them in.

2.2 The content of the questionnaires

The main topics covered in the questionnaires for pupils were:

- **background variables** including: gender; surrogate measures intended to provide an approximate indication of the cultural level of the home (e.g. the approximate number of books in the home; and daily newspapers read by parents); perceived ability and behaviour in school; and post-16 educational intentions;

- **attitudes towards school and learning** including: views about the value of school and school work; liking for school; interest and boredom with school work; and opinions on the purposes of schooling;

- **perceptions of teachers and lessons** including: liking for teachers; teachers' support of pupils' learning; teachers' maintenance of discipline; individual discussions with teachers about school work; and liking for different types of lessons;

- **pupils' self-reported behaviour in and out of school** including: behaviour in school; punishments; truancy; participation in lunch hour or after school activities; reading for pleasure; length of time spent doing homework, watching television or videos, and playing computer games;

- **perceptions of parental interest and home support** including: parents' opinions about the value of education; parental interest in pupils' progress at school; parental encouragement of good behaviour in school.

The pupils' questionnaire consisted of two main types of question. In the first part of the questionnaire pupils were asked to indicate their level of agreement with each of a number of statements by circling a number on a five-point scale, either:

agree a lot/ agree/ not sure/ disagree/ disagree a lot;
or
all lessons/ most lessons/ some lessons/ hardly any lessons/ no lessons;
or
always/ nearly always/ sometimes/ hardly ever/ never

as appropriate to the content of the statement.

Most of the remainder of the questionnaire consisted of 'closed' questions which required pupils to select one or more pre-coded responses by circling a number or ticking a box. At the end of the questionnaire pupils were invited to write their own comments about their school.

The main topics covered in the questionnaires for schools were:

- **background information** including: type of catchment area; percentages of pupils receiving free school meals and from ethnic minorities; and the approximate proportion of the intake with reading ages more than two years behind in chronological ages;

- **consultation, reviewing and recording procedures** used to support pupils' progress.

Most of the questions in the school questionnaire asked schools either to enter a number or a percentage in a box or to select one or more pre-coded responses by circling a number or a tick.

2.3 Sampling, administration and response rates

The samples of schools for each age group were drawn from schools in England and Wales containing pupils of that age group. The schools were randomly selected from the Register of Schools, an annually updated database of all schools in England and Wales maintained by the NFER. The samples of schools for each age group were stratified by size (in terms of the numbers of pupils in the relevant age group), type of school (infant and junior, junior and independent for the top primary sample; comprehensive to 16, comprehensive to 18, other secondary and independent for the first-year secondary sample), region (North, Midlands, South) and type of LEA (metropolitan, non-metropolitan). Middle schools were excluded from both samples since the study set out to investigate whether any differences in the attitudes towards school of pupils in their final year of primary schooling and pupils in their first year at secondary school were related to differences between primary and secondary schools.

It was intended to achieve samples of about 1250 top primary pupils and 1000 first-year secondary pupils. A slightly larger sample of top primary pupils was required, as it was planned to re-survey the same pupils one year later to gain data concerning how, if at all, the views of these pupils changed when they moved to secondary school; the larger sample was required to allow for attrition affecting the follow-up survey.

A total of 85 schools was selected for the top primary sample and 80 schools for the first-year secondary sample; this represented approximately twice the number of schools required to achieve the totals of 1250 and 1000 pupils from the primary and secondary samples respectively. Previous experience had shown that roughly a 50 per cent response rate could be expected; hence twice the number of schools required were originally contacted.

The response rate from schools was, in fact, very positive, to the extent that six primary and six secondary schools who were willing to take part in the survey had to be refused as all the questionnaires available had already been allocated to schools. Overall, the achieved sample consisted of 1265 top primary pupils in 38 schools and 1009 first-year secondary pupils in 41 schools. In addition to the questionnaires completed by pupils, headteachers were asked to arrange for the completion of a short school background questionnaire. Their responses are described in Appendix 1.

The survey was administered by NFER's Field Research Services Department in summer 1994. All schools selected for the samples were invited to take part in the study. In the case of the primary schools, all pupils in the top year group were surveyed, whereas for the secondary schools one tutor group was randomly selected by NFER from the list of first-year secondary tutor groups supplied by the school. One written reminder and (where appropriate) a subsequent telephone reminder was given to schools concerning the return of the completed questionnaires to the NFER. Tables A2.1 and A2.2 provide full details of the numbers of schools contacted, reasons for refusing to participate and numbers of questionnaires dispatched and returned.

The data were analysed by the NFER's Statistics Department, using the SPSSX statistical package. In order to reduce any bias due to non-response, the samples were weighted to reflect the national distribution of pupils in terms of school type (infant and junior, junior and independent, for top primary pupils; comprehensive, independent, others, for first-year secondary pupils), area (metropolitan; non-metropolitan) and region (North; Midlands; South).

CHAPTER 3

A COMPARISON OF THE RESPONSES OF TOP PRIMARY AND FIRST-YEAR SECONDARY PUPILS

3.1   Introduction

The central issue being investigated in this study concerned the proportion of pupils who held negative attitudes towards school. The previous NFER study (Keys and Fernandes, 1993) had identified a substantial minority of first-year secondary (Year 7) pupils holding negative attitudes towards school. This finding raised the important question of whether these attitudes had developed during their first year of secondary education, or whether the pupils concerned had already formed them during their years of primary schooling. The research documented in this chapter was initiated to compare the attitudes towards school and education of samples of top primary (Year 6) and first-year secondary (Year 7) pupils. The key questions that the study set out to answer were:

♦   Were there any differences in the proportions of the top primary and first-year secondary pupils holding negative attitudes towards school and education?

♦   What were the similarities and differences between the attitudes towards school and education of top primary and first-year secondary school pupils?

The pupils' responses to the questionnaires have been grouped into the following main categories:

● attitudes toward school and learning

● perceptions of teachers, teaching and discipline

● pupils' self-reported ability and behaviour

● perceptions of parental support

● pupils' aspirations for their future

● pupils' comments on their schools.

Throughout this chapter the comparisons between top primary and first-year secondary pupils' responses have normally been made by combining the two positive responses 'agree a lot' and 'agree' and by similarly combining the two negative responses 'disagree a lot' and 'disagree'. In a few instances, if considered appropriate, comparisons are made in terms of the proportions of each group selecting the most positive ('agree a lot') or most negative ('disagree a lot') response. The chi-square test has been used to determine the statistical significance of any differences between the two samples. The five per cent level of statistical significance has been accepted as evidence of difference between the two groups. However, because of the large size of the samples, differences of a few percentage points were found to be statistically significant at the five per cent, or even the one per cent, level. Differences of this size, even if statistically significant, may not be particularly interesting from an educational point of view. We have therefore tried to identify patterns within the data, i.e. sets of statements focusing on one issue (for example, like and dislike of school) for which the patterns of response were similar.

3.2 Attitudes towards school and learning

The pupils in both age groups were asked to indicate their attitudes towards school and school work by responding to specific statements focusing on:

- like and dislike of school
- interest in and boredom with school work
- perceptions of the value of school, school work and the local reputation of their school
- the purposes of schooling.

3.2.1 Like and dislike of school

The pupils' responses to the three statements concerned with like and dislike of school are shown in Table 3.1.

The study revealed a very positive picture with regard to pupils' liking for school. Nearly three-quarters of both the Year 6 (top primary) and Year 7 (first-year secondary) pupils indicated that they were happy at school ('agree a lot' or 'agree'). *And,* when asked to respond to the statement 'On the whole I like being at school', an even more positive response was found, with more than eight out of ten pupils in each year group either agreeing or agreeing a lot.

However, small minorities of pupils in both age groups appeared to hold negative attitudes. About seven to eight per cent of the top primary pupils and 10 – 13 per cent of those in the first year of secondary school 'disagreed' or 'disagreed a lot' with these two statements (i.e. disliked school).

Our results also suggest that the top primary pupils tend to hold slightly more positive attitudes than those in the first year of secondary school. For both statements the primary school pupils were more likely than those in the secondary school to select the most positive option 'agree a lot' (17 per cent compared with 12 per cent; and 30 per cent compared with 23 per cent). However, it is worth exercising caution in the interpretation of these results, since it could simply be an artefact of the fact that the older pupils have become more discerning and less willing to express extreme levels of enthusiasm (Keys and Fernandes, 1993).

Table 3.1   Likes and dislike of school: the responses of top primary (Year 6) and first-year secondary pupils (Year 7) compared

	primary		secondary	
Total.........	1265	100%	1009	100%
I am very happy when I am at school				
Agree a lot	214	16.9%	121	12.0%
Agree...	714	56.4%	604	59.9%
Not sure	242	19.2%	153	15.2%
Disagree	68	5.4%	100	9.9%
Disagree a lot...	21	1.7%	29	2.8%
Missing	6	.5%	1	.1%
On the whole I like being at school				
Agree a lot	382	30.2%	228	22.6%
Agree...	646	51.0%	601	59.6%
Not sure	140	11.1%	80	8.0%
Disagree	68	5.4%	61	6.1%
Disagree a lot...	26	2.1%	36	3.6%
Missing	3	.2%	2	.2%
Most of the time I don't want to go to school				
Agree a lot	122	9.7%	98	9.7%
Agree...	245	19.4%	264	26.2%
Not sure	152	12.0%	93	9.3%
Disagree	453	35.8%	373	37.0%
Disagree a lot...	286	22.6%	177	17.5%
Missing	7	.6%	3	.3%

When presented with a negative statement, the proportions of pupils in both year groups who disagreed with the statement 'Most of the time I don't want to go to school' (i.e. who expressed a favourable attitude) were considerably smaller than those who had shown favourable attitudes on the two previous statements. About 58 per cent of the top primary pupils and 55 per cent of the secondary pupils disagreed with the statement. Once again, the top primary pupils were more likely to opt for the most positive option (23 per cent, compared with 18 per cent of those in the secondary school, disagreed a lot with this statement). The secondary pupils were more likely to opt for the negative options (36 per cent compared with 29 per cent of the top primary pupils agreed or agreed a lot with the statement that most of the time they did not want to go to school). Although at first sight this may seem to be a cause for concern, it is possible that some of the pupils making this negative response did not actively dislike school but simply preferred pursuing other interests or activities.

3.2.2 Interest or boredom in lessons

Three statements in the questionnaire were designed to measure pupils' levels of interest, or boredom, in lessons (Table 3.2).

Table 3.2   Interest or boredom in lessons: the responses of top primary and first-year secondary pupils compared

	primary		secondary	
Total.........	1265	100%	1009	100%
The work I do in lessons is interesting to me				
All lessons..	240	19.0%	133	13.2%
Most lessons	593	46.9%	499	49.4%
Some lessons..	365	28.9%	328	32.5%
Hardly any lessons	46	3.6%	31	3.1%
No lessons	12	.9%	15	1.5%
Missing	9	.7%	3	.3%
I am bored in lessons				
All lessons..	32	2.5%	21	2.1%
Most lessons	67	5.3%	62	6.1%
Some lessons..	527	41.7%	466	46.1%
Hardly any lessons	456	36.0%	383	37.9%
No lessons	175	13.9%	78	7.7%
Missing	8	.6%	–	–
In a lesson, I often count the minutes till breaktime				
All lessons..	202	16.0%	86	8.6%
Most lessons	184	14.6%	129	12.8%
Some lessons..	374	29.5%	382	37.8%
Hardly any lessons	283	22.4%	253	25.1%
No lessons	218	17.2%	157	15.5%
Missing	4	.3%	2	.2%

A higher proportion of top primary pupils said they found 'all lessons' interesting (19 per cent compared with 13 per cent of first-year secondary pupils). However, when the proportions finding all and most lessons interesting were combined, the difference became smaller (66 per cent compared with 63 per cent of the secondary pupils). The proportions of pupils who were interested in 'hardly any lessons' or 'no lessons' were the same (five per cent) for both year groups.

About half of the pupils in both year groups indicated that they were never or hardly ever bored in lessons; the top primary pupils were more likely to express the most positive view (14 per cent compared with eight per cent of the secondary pupils indicated that they were never bored in lessons). Very few pupils (eight per cent in both year groups) said that they found all or most lessons boring, although just over 40 per cent in both groups admitted to boredom in some lessons.

The responses of the primary pupils were slightly less positive than those of the secondary school pupils to the statement 'I often count the minutes till break-time'; about 30 per cent of the primary pupils, compared with about 20 per cent of those in the secondary school, said that they often counted the minutes towards the end in all lessons. Possible reasons for this include younger pupils having a shorter attention span, together with the fact that primary schools generally have more flexible lesson timings, whereas secondary schools usually timetable lessons in approximately 30-minute periods (or one-hour 'doubles').

It is worth remembering at this point that the two samples of pupils were likely to have experienced different types of teaching. The top primary pupils were likely to be taught most, if not all, subjects by one class teacher. On the other hand, the pupils in their first year at secondary school would have been taught different subjects by different subject teachers. This means that first-year secondary pupils had more opportunities to experience different teachers' teaching styles, possibly finding that some teachers made the work more interesting.

In general, the differences between the responses of the two year groups to the set of statements concerned with interest in school work were less marked than those between their responses to the statements concerned with liking for school. Nevertheless, there appears to have been a slight tendency for the top primary pupils to express more positive attitudes than those in the first year of secondary school. However, as noted above, this may have been because the younger pupils were less discriminating and more willing to express positive views.

3.2.3 The value of school and school work

Three statements were designed to elicit pupils' views on the value of school and school work. Pupils' responses are shown in Table 3.3.

Table 3.3 The value of school and school work: the responses of top primary and first-year secondary pupils compared

	primary		secondary	
Total.........	1265	100%	1009	100%
School work is worth doing				
Agree a lot	569	45.0%	389	38.5%
Agree	589	46.5%	545	54.0%
Not sure	60	4.7%	25	2.5%
Disagree	19	1.5%	23	2.3%
Disagree a lot	20	1.6%	21	2.1%
Missing	9	.7%	6	.6%
The work I do in lessons is a waste of time				
All lessons	21	1.6%	8	.8%
Most lessons	27	2.1%	16	1.6%
Some lessons	128	10.2%	115	11.4%
Hardly any lessons	325	25.7%	326	32.4%
No lessons	751	59.4%	535	53.0%
Missing	13	1.0%	8	.8%
School is a waste of time for me				
Agree a lot	17	1.3%	8	.8%
Agree	20	1.6%	23	2.3%
Not sure	59	4.7%	41	4.0%
Disagree	300	23.7%	307	30.4%
Disagree a lot	864	68.3%	628	62.2%
Missing	5	.4%	2	.2%

The majority of top primary and lower secondary pupils responded positively to the statement 'School work is worth doing', with totals of 92 per cent and 93 per cent agreeing respectively. Furthermore, the proportions of each sample expressing a negative view towards school work were small (three per cent in the primary school sample and four per cent in the secondary).

However, while the total responding positively was virtually the same for both samples, the primary school pupils were inclined to be more positive, agreeing a lot with the statement rather than just agreeing (45 per cent compared with 39 per cent in the secondary school).

Pupils were also asked to respond to two negative statements: 'The work I do in lessons is a waste of time' and, at a more general level, 'School is a waste of time for me'. The finding that a majority of pupils disagreed with these statements would seem to confirm the trend indicated above. It is very encouraging to find that a significant majority of pupils in both year groups rejected the view that the work they did in lessons was a waste of time. About 85 per cent of the pupils in both year groups opted for the two most positive options (i.e. agreeing that the work they did in lessons was never/hardly ever a waste of time). Similarly, over 90 per cent of both samples disagreed with the statement 'School is a waste of time for me'. Only about three per cent of pupils from each sample agreed with these two statements (i.e. held negative views about the value of school and school work).

Once again, however, the responses from primary school pupils were slightly more positive, with about 59 per cent reporting that 'no lessons' were a waste of time, as compared with 53 per cent of those in the secondary school. Similarly, slightly more top primary pupils 'disagreed a lot' with the statement 'School is a waste of time for me' as compared with the secondary pupils (68 per cent and 62 per cent respectively).

3.2.4 Pupils' perceptions of the purposes of school

Five statements focused on the long-term purposes of school. Table 3.4 shows the pupils' response to each statement.

Pupils' responses to the statement 'Schools should help us to do as well as possible in tests and exams (like GCSE)' showed that the proportions of top primary and lower secondary pupils agreeing with the statement were very similar (95 per cent and 97 per cent respectively). Very few pupils in either age group disagreed with the statement or indicated that they were 'not sure'. However, the secondary pupils were more likely than the primary school pupils to 'agree a lot' (77 per cent and 67 per cent respectively), suggesting that the older pupils, even after only one year at secondary school, had become more aware of the importance of doing well in examinations.

Table 3.4 Pupils' perceptions of the purposes of school: the responses of top primary and first-year secondary pupils compared

	primary		secondary	
Total.........	1265	100%	1009	100%
Schools should help us to do as well as possible in tests and in exams (like GCSE)				
Agree a lot	847	67.0%	780	77.3%
Agree..	357	28.2%	202	20.0%
Not sure	31	2.5%	15	1.5%
Disagree	17	1.3%	7	.7%
Disagree a lot	9	.7%	2	.2%
Missing	3	.2%	4	.4%
Schools should teach things that will be useful when we get jobs				
Agree a lot	854	67.5%	728	72.2%
Agree..	322	25.5%	249	24.6%
Not sure	52	4.1%	21	2.1%
Disagree	24	1.9%	9	.9%
Disagree a lot	3	.2%	1	.1%
Missing	10	.8%	–	–
Schools should help me to be independent and stand on my own two feet				
Agree a lot	576	45.5%	423	41.9%
Agree..	512	40.5%	487	48.3%
Not sure	101	7.9%	61	6.1%
Disagree	44	3.5%	32	3.2%
Disagree a lot	19	1.5%	5	.5%
Missing	13	1.0%	1	.1%
Schools should help us to learn how to use our spare/leisure time				
Agree a lot	266	21.1%	151	15.0%
Agree..	441	34.9%	365	36.2%
Not sure	239	18.9%	130	12.8%
Disagree	204	16.1%	244	24.2%
Disagree a lot	108	8.5%	117	11.6%
Missing	6	.5%	2	.2%
School work doesn't help you get a job				
Agree a lot	31	2.4%	19	1.8%
Agree..	42	3.3%	26	2.5%
Not sure	72	5.7%	38	3.8%
Disagree	276	21.8%	264	26.2%
Disagree a lot	836	66.1%	661	65.5%
Missing	8	.6%	2	.2%

The statement 'Schools should teach things that will be useful when we get jobs' prompted very similar reactions from both age groups. Again, a considerable majority agreed with the statement (93 per cent of the primary pupils and 97 per cent of those in secondary school), while the proportion agreeing a lot was higher amongst the secondary school pupils (72 per cent compared with 68 per cent of the primary school pupils).

The majority of pupils in both age groups agreed that 'Schools should help me to be independent and stand on my own two feet' (86 per cent of the primary pupils and 90 per cent of those in secondary school) and very few pupils (five per cent of the primary pupils and four per cent of the secondary) disagreed with this statement.

Interestingly, the proportion of pupils who 'agreed a lot' that schools should help them to become independent was slightly higher amongst the top primary pupils than amongst those in the first year of secondary school (46 per cent compared with 42 per cent), whereas the combined percentage ('agree a lot' plus 'agree') was slightly higher for the secondary pupils (see above).

Although the majority of pupils from both age groups agreed with the statement 'Schools should help us to learn how to spend our spare/leisure time', the proportions were considerably less than had agreed with the statements concerned with passing examinations, getting jobs and becoming independent. About half of all the pupils agreed with the statement, although in both age groups more pupils had selected 'agree' rather than 'agree a lot'. However, 36 per cent of the secondary pupils, compared with a quarter of those in the primary schools, disagreed with the statement (i.e. they did not agree that schools should help them to learn how to use their leisure time). In addition, the secondary pupils were less likely to opt for 'agree a lot' (15 per cent compared with 21 per cent of those in the primary school).

The proportions of pupils who selected the option 'not sure' were greater than for the other three statements above: 19 per cent of the primary pupils and 13 per cent of the secondary. Overall, the pupils' responses suggest that considerable numbers of pupils did not feel that schools should help them to learn how to spend their spare time, with the secondary pupils believing that schools had a less significant role in this respect than did the primary pupils.

The majority of pupils were clearly convinced of the value of school work in helping them to get a job. A sizeable majority at both age groups disagreed with the statement 'School work doesn't help me to get a job' (88 per cent of primary and 92 per cent of secondary pupils). Many of the pupils chose the most extreme response 'disagree a lot' (approximately two-thirds of each age group), suggesting they were well aware of the role of school work in helping them to get jobs when they left school. Only a small proportion of pupils were unconvinced of the value of school work (six per cent of primary and four per cent of secondary pupils).

3.2.5 Perceived reputation of their school

Pupils were asked to respond to two statements relating to the reputation of their school. Their views are shown in Table 3.5.

Table 3.5 Perceived reputation of their school: the responses of top primary and first-year secondary pupils compared

	primary		secondary	
Total.........	1265	100%	1009	100%
People think this is a good school				
Agree a lot	535	42.3%	387	38.4%
Agree	511	40.4%	482	47.8%
Not sure	148	11.7%	95	9.4%
Disagree	37	2.9%	32	3.2%
Disagree a lot	21	1.7%	11	1.1%
Missing	13	1.0%	2	.2%
My school is clean and tidy				
Always	503	39.8%	194	19.2%
Nearly always	551	43.5%	503	49.9%
Sometimes...	174	13.7%	222	22.0%
Hardly ever	14	1.1%	44	4.4%
Never..	20	1.6%	40	4.0%
Missing	4	.3%	5	.5%

The proportions of pupils who thought their school was well-regarded were very similar for each age group (83 per cent of the primary pupils and 86 per cent of the secondary).

There was a considerable difference, however, in the responses to the statement 'My school is clean and tidy'. More than twice as many primary pupils as secondary school pupils agreed that this was 'always' the case (40 per cent and 19 per cent respectively) and even when the proportions selecting the two positive options ('always' and 'nearly always') were combined, the responses of the primary school pupils remained more positive (83 per cent compared with 69 per cent of those in the secondary school agreed that their school was always/nearly always clean and tidy).

When we compare the percentages with those reported in the earlier study (Keys and Fernandes, op. cit.), which focused on Year 7 and Year 9 secondary school students, two interesting points emerge:

- ◆ The percentage of Year 7 students responding most positively ('My school is always clean and tidy') was roughly the same in both studies (19 per cent in this study and 18 per cent in the previous study).

- ◆ The proportions selecting the most positive option ('My school is always clean and tidy') appears to decrease with age (40 per cent for Year 6 (primary) in this study; 19 per cent and 18 per cent for Year 7 in this study and the previous study, respectively; and nine per cent for Year 9 in the previous study).

There are several possible reasons for the differences between the responses of primary and secondary school pupils: primary schools are usually much smaller than secondary schools and may therefore be easier to keep clean and tidy; primary school pupils are usually taught predominantly in one teaching area, whereas secondary school pupils move to different teaching areas for different subjects. Secondary pupils are therefore more likely to see more different areas of the school during the course of a week; and more pupil movement about the school may provide more opportunities for litter to be dropped or equipment to be left out of place. Younger pupils are frequently eager to help tidy up teaching areas, whereas older pupils are often less inclined to do so. Also, the culture of the primary school may place more emphasis on displaying work on classroom walls and involving children in the care of garden areas, etc.

However, it is not clear why the responses of Year 9 students should be less positive than those of Year 7 since in most cases they were in the same types of schools. The less positive response of the Year 9 students may simply have reflected their overall less positive attitudes towards school.

3.3   Teachers, teaching and discipline

Pupils were asked for their views on teachers, teaching and discipline within class. They were provided with specific statements concerning:
- ● liking for teachers
- ● teacher support for pupils' learning
- ● the maintenance of discipline

3.3.1. Liking for teachers

Pupils were asked to respond to the statement 'I like my teacher' (for primary school pupils, who would usually have one class teacher for most, if not all lessons), or 'I like my teachers' (for the secondary pupils, since they would usually be taught by different teachers for different subjects). It should be borne in mind, therefore, that the responses of the two age groups are not directly comparable and that this fact may well explain some of the differences found. Pupils' responses are shown in Table 3.6.

Table 3.6 Liking for teachers: the responses of top primary and first-year secondary pupils compared

	primary		secondary	
Total.........	1265	100%	1009	100%
I like my teacher(s)				
Always	540	42.7%	155	15.4%
Nearly always	373	29.5%	384	38.1%
Sometimes.....................................	254	20.1%	395	39.2%
Hardly ever	45	3.5%	46	4.6%
Never...	46	3.6%	28	2.8%
Missing	6	.5%	–	–

The responses of the primary school pupils were far more positive than those of the pupils in the first year of secondary school: almost three times as many primary pupils reported that they 'always' liked their teacher (43 per cent compared with 15 per cent of the secondary pupils). Even when the proportions selecting 'always' and 'nearly always' were combined, the difference between the two groups was quite large (72 per cent of the primary pupils, compared with 54 per cent of those in the secondary school, always or nearly always liked their teacher(s)).

Although these responses seem to suggest that secondary school pupils were far less positive than top primary school pupils about their liking for their teacher(s), it should be borne in mind that the difference in school organisation at primary and secondary levels may be a significant factor influencing these responses. Most primary school pupils will have spent each year of primary schooling with one class teacher, a situation in which it would be possible to develop close pupil-teacher relationships. On entering secondary school, however, pupils will have had different teachers for specific subjects; with the exception of their form tutor, it is likely that pupils would see most teachers for a very small proportion of the total school week, thus making it difficult to establish the same level of familiarity with any secondary school teacher as was possible with primary school teachers.

It may be of interest here to note that the proportion of pupils indicating that they never/hardly ever liked their teachers was the same (seven per cent) for both groups.

3.3.2 Ensuring the quality of pupils' work

Pupils were asked to respond to four statements relating to strategies that teachers use to ensure the quality of pupils' work. There were minor differences between the primary and secondary versions of the statements, which reflected the fact that secondary school pupils are normally taught by different teachers, whilst primary school pupils are normally taught by one class teacher. Table 3.7 shows pupils' responses.

Table 3.7 Ensuring the quality of pupils' work: the responses of top primary and first-year secondary pupils compared

	primary		secondary	
Total.........	1265	100%	1009	100%
My teacher(s):				
always marks my work	719	56.9%	363	36.0%
usually marks my work	512	40.5%	595	59.0%
hardly ever marks my work	29	2.3%	49	4.8%
Missing	5	.4%	2	.2%
My teacher(s) makes sure we do any homework that is set				
Always	787	62.2%	575	57.0%
Nearly always	291	23.0%	358	35.5%
Sometimes...	124	9.8%	57	5.7%
Hardly ever	25	2.0%	13	1.3%
Never...	22	1.8%	6	.6%
Missing	15	1.2%	–	–
My teacher(s):				
tries hard to make me work as well as I am able ...	1082	85.5%	779	77.2%
is fairly easily satisfied	166	13.1%	208	20.6%
doesn't seem to care whether I work or not	12	1.0%	19	1.8%
Missing	5	.4%	4	.4%
My teacher(s) tells me when I do my school work well				
Always	623	49.2%	457	45.3%
Nearly always	409	32.3%	383	38.0%
Sometimes...	194	15.4%	125	12.4%
Hardly ever	19	1.5%	32	3.2%
Never...	15	1.2%	9	.9%
Missing	5	.4%	2	.2%

The overall picture, as indicated by pupils' responses to the four statements shown in Table 3.7, was one of the majority of teachers regularly monitoring pupils' work and taking steps to motivate pupils.

About 97 per cent of primary school pupils indicated that their teacher always or usually marked their work as compared with 95 per cent of those in the secondary school. However, a higher proportion of primary pupils said that their teachers 'always mark my work' (57 per cent as compared with 36 per cent of secondary). For both samples, the percentage who indicated their teachers 'hardly ever mark my work' was very low (three per cent and five per cent for primary and secondary respectively).

Although at first sight it could be worrying that only about one-third of first-year secondary school pupils reported that their work was 'always' marked, it is likely that, for some subjects at least, pupils may have been asked to swap books and mark each other's work in class. Also, some types of homework set, such as reading or researching a particular subject, do not lend themselves to being marked.

The pupils' responses suggest that most teachers checked to see that homework had been done. The majority of all pupils indicated that their teachers 'always' made sure that pupils did any homework that was set (63 per cent of primary and 57 per cent of secondary – a slight difference in favour of primary). However, when the proportions opting for 'always' and 'nearly always' were combined, slightly more of the secondary pupils responded positively (93 per cent compared with 86 per cent in the primary school).

In terms of encouraging and motivating pupils, the majority of pupils at both age groups indicated that 'My teacher(s) tries hard to make me work as well as I can', although the responses of the primary school pupils were slightly more positive (86 per cent compared with 77 per cent of the secondary). In addition, rather more secondary school pupils felt that their teachers were 'fairly easily satisfied' (21 per cent compared with 13 per cent of those in the primary school). It is interesting to note that the responses from Year 7 pupils in the previous study were virtually identical to the responses from the secondary pupils in this study ('try hard to make me work as well as I am able' 71 per cent; 'fairly easily satisfied' 25 per cent; and 'don't seem to care whether I work or not' three per cent, for the previous study).

Overall, responses from both groups of pupils showed that most teachers told them when they did their work well. About 82 per cent of primary pupils and 84 per cent of first-year secondary pupils reported that their teachers 'always' or 'nearly always' told them when they produced good work. However, the primary school pupils were more likely to indicate that their teacher 'always' told them when they did their school work well (49 per cent compared with 45 per cent of those in the secondary school). Very few pupils indicated that they were 'hardly ever' or 'never' told (three per cent of primary and four per cent of secondary). It is not possible to make direct comparisons with the earlier study since the wording was changed from 'my teachers *praise* me...' in the earlier study to 'my teachers *tell* me...' in the current study.

3.3.3 Maintaining discipline

The issue of discipline within schools is an important one and many people would argue that without discipline it is difficult to provide an effective learning environment. Six statements focused on different aspects of discipline within the school generally and within classes. Table 3.8 shows pupils' responses.

The responses from the top primary and first-year secondary pupils were fairly similar for the first statement. About 64 per cent of pupils in both groups indicated that their teachers 'always' took action when they saw anyone breaking school rules. Most of the remainder indicated that teachers 'nearly always' took action. These responses suggest that, in the eyes of top primary and first-year secondary pupils, teachers were rigorous in enforcing school rules.

Responses from both samples of pupils also indicated that teachers made it clear how pupils should behave in school. About three-quarters of pupils in each age group reported that their teachers 'always' made clear their behavioural expectations (78 per cent in primary and 74 per cent in secondary – indicating a slightly more positive response from the primary school pupils). Most of the remaining pupils in both year groups indicated that their teachers 'nearly always' made it clear how pupils should behave.

Evidently, the vast majority of teachers made it clear to pupils how they should behave in school and took action when they saw anyone breaking school rules. It is also worth noting the consensus in the views of both age groups. Pupils' views regarding their teachers' abilities to control classes were, however, noticeably different for the primary and secondary samples.

About 55 per cent of top primary pupils reported that their teachers could 'always' control the class, more than twice as many as the secondary pupils (24 per cent). Even when the proportions opting for 'always' and 'nearly always' were combined, the responses of the primary pupils were more positive (85 per cent, compared with 70 per cent of the secondary pupils, reported that teachers could always or nearly always control the class).

Pupils from both age groups appeared to recognise the importance of school rules and felt that their own school had an appropriate code. About 87 per cent of primary pupils and 85 per cent of secondary pupils agreed with the statement 'My school has sensible rules', although a higher proportion of the younger pupils 'agreed a lot' (38 per cent compared with 27 per cent of the older year group) and a slightly larger proportion of the secondary pupils chose to disagree with the statement (seven per cent of primary and nine per cent of secondary).

Table 3.8 Maintaining discipline: the responses of top primary and first-year secondary pupils compared

	primary		secondary	
Total.........	1265	100%	1009	100%
The teachers in my school take action when they see anyone breaking school rules				
Always	808	63.9%	641	63.6%
Nearly always	339	26.8%	295	29.2%
Sometimes..	83	6.5%	59	5.8%
Hardly ever	22	1.7%	10	1.0%
Never..	8	.6%	3	.3%
Missing	5	.4%	1	.1%
My teacher(s) makes it clear how we should behave in school				
Always	983	77.7%	742	73.6%
Nearly always	202	16.0%	211	21.0%
Sometimes..	57	4.5%	50	4.9%
Hardly ever	9	.7%	3	.3%
Never..	9	.7%	1	.1%
Missing	6	.5%	1	.1%
My teacher(s) can control the class				
Always	693	54.8%	240	23.8%
Nearly always	372	29.4%	461	45.7%
Sometimes..	139	11.0%	238	23.6%
Hardly ever	28	2.2%	42	4.1%
Never..	28	2.2%	25	2.5%
Missing	5	.4%	4	.4%
My school has sensible rules				
Agree a lot	484	38.3%	273	27.1%
Agree..	611	48.3%	581	57.6%
Not sure	84	6.6%	63	6.2%
Disagree	74	5.8%	76	7.6%
Disagree a lot..	10	.8%	15	1.5%
Missing	2	.1%	1.	.1%

	primary		secondary	
Do you think the discipline in your school is:				
too strict?	64	5.0%	130	12.9%
about right?...	1143	90.4%	831	82.3%
not strict enough?	48	3.8%	45	4.5%
Missing	10	.8%	2	.2%
Does your school have:				
too many rules?...	191	15.1%	258	25.6%
about the right number of rules?	1001	79.1%	716	70.9%
not enough rules?	65	5.2%	32	3.2%
Missing	8	.6%	3	.3%

Whilst there were mixed views on school rules and teachers' abilities to control classes, it was very clear that the vast majority of pupils considered that the level of discipline within the school was 'about right', although primary pupils were slightly more likely to express positive views (90 per cent of primary pupils chose this option, compared with 82 per cent of the secondary pupils). More than twice as many of the older pupils felt that the discipline within the school was 'too strict' compared with the top primary pupils (13 per cent and five per cent respectively). Fewer than five per cent at each age group considered that discipline was 'not strict enough'.

The final question relating to discipline matters concerned the number of school rules. Again, the majority of pupils from both samples indicated that their school had 'about the right number of rules', although primary pupils were slightly more likely to express positive views (79 per cent compared with 71 per cent of the secondary pupils). A quarter of the older pupils, compared with only 15 per cent of the younger pupils, felt that the school had too many rules.

In this context, it should be borne in mind that pupils in their first year of secondary schooling would be likely to reflect on, and contrast, the systems in primary and secondary schools. By virtue of their size and age range, secondary schools are more likely to have more rules than primary schools: the contrast between the two sectors is probably most apparent to pupils who have recently transferred from the primary to the secondary phase. It is therefore not surprising that one in four first-year secondary pupils considered the school to have too many rules.

The last three statements discussed above all relate to pupils' perceptions of the whole-school ethos, in terms of rules and the approach to discipline. When we compare the responses of the secondary pupils in this study to those in the previous survey, we find they are broadly similar for these three statements.

The Year 9 students in the previous study were, however, more likely to disagree with the statement 'My school has sensible rules' (23 per cent 'disagree' and five per cent 'strongly disagree'). In addition, far more Year 9 students felt that the school had 'too many rules' (40 per cent). These data are included as they help to illustrate a trend whereby, as pupils get older (move to higher year groups), the proportions who consider the school has too many rules and who disagree with the statement 'My school has sensible rules' increase. This may be evidence that more rules are applied to older pupils, or it may be indicative of an increasing resistance to 'authority' or 'the establishment' as evidenced in school rules.

3.3.4 Talking individually to teachers

Discussions between individual pupils and their teachers can be a useful strategy for monitoring progress and motivation and setting future targets. Questions concerning this were presented in different formats for the primary and secondary pupils: for the primary pupils the question focused on discussions with the pupil's class teacher; for the secondary pupils the question asked about discussions with the pupil's form teacher **and** any other teacher. Table 3.9 shows pupils' responses.

Table 3.9 Talking individually to teachers: the responses of top primary and first-year secondary pupils compared

	primary		secondary	
Total.........	1265	100%	1009	100%
Have you talked to your class teacher about your work this year?				
Yes, often	108	8.5%	80	8.0%
Yes, sometimes	476	37.6%	419	41.5%
No, never...	676	53.4%	486	48.2%
Missing	5	.4%	24	2.4%
Have you talked to other teachers about your work?				
Yes, often	NA	NA	79	7.9%
Yes, sometimes	NA	NA	406	40.3%
No, never...	NA	NA	504	49.9%
Missing	NA	NA	20	1.9%

According to the pupils' responses, fewer than one in ten of pupils at either age group 'often' talked to his/her class teacher (form teacher for the secondary pupils). About half of the pupils at both age groups asserted that they 'never' had individual discussions about how well they were doing at school (54 per cent of primary and 49 per cent of secondary). The proportions of secondary pupils who talked on a one-to-one basis with teachers other than their form teacher were almost the same as were reported for individual discussions with the form teacher.

Whilst at first sight it appears very disturbing that so few pupils frequently have individual discussions about their work with their teachers, it is possible that different interpretations of the type of situation referred to have influenced responses. For example, a pupil who interpreted the statement as referring to a very formal situation, away from the rest of the class, might consider s/he had 'never' had this type of discussion with her/his teacher. Conversely, a pupil who interpreted the statement rather more loosely, in terms of comments by and dialogue with the teacher during lessons, might consider s/he had often had discussions about work. It is also worth remembering that, although teachers may be convinced of the value of discussions with individual pupils, there have been numerous additional demands on their time in recent years. This may have had the effect of reducing the time available for formal, one-to-one discussions with pupils. Clearly this area merits further investigation. However, even if the perceptions of the pupils taking part in our study are not entirely accurate, schools should be aware that many pupils believed that they had very few opportunities for one-to-one discussion with their teachers.

3.3.5. Types of lesson liked

Four statements were presented, suggesting different types of lesson that might be experienced in primary and secondary schools. Pupils' responses to the statements are shown in Table 3.10.

The two most popular types of lesson for both age groups were those where pupils could work with their friends and those where pupils could make something. More than nine out of ten pupils from both groups agreed with the statement 'I like lessons where I can work with my friends' (92 per cent and 96 per cent respectively). Similar proportions of pupils agreed with the statement 'I like lessons where I can make something' (92 per cent of primary and 92 per cent of secondary).

Lessons where pupils talked about their ideas were liked by roughly eight out of ten pupils, again with very similar numbers for each age group (77 per cent of primary and 80 per cent of secondary). However, for both groups, fewer pupils chose the more positive response 'agree a lot' as compared with simply 'agree', whereas for the two statements discussed above, the majority of pupils chose the more positive option.

Of all four lesson types outlined, the one which was least widely liked was lessons in which pupils worked on their own. About half the pupils in both groups agreed that they liked this type of lesson; conversely roughly one-third of each age group reported that they disliked working on their own.

Table 3.10 Types of lessons liked: the responses of top primary and first year secondary pupils compared

	primary		secondary	
Total.........	1265	100%	1009	100%
I like lessons where I can work with my friends				
Agree a lot	832	65.8%	628	62.2%
Agree..	334	26.4%	336	33.3%
Not sure	42	3.3%	18	1.8%
Disagree	25	2.0%	21	2.0%
Disagree a lot	27	2.1%	5	.5%
Missing	5	.4%	2	.2%
I like lessons where I can work on my own				
Agree a lot	234	18.5%	138	13.7%
Agree..	425	33.6%	412	40.8%
Not sure	199	15.7%	103	10.2%
Disagree	245	19.4%	228	22.6%
Disagree a lot	154	12.2%	125	12.4%
Missing	8	.6%	3	.3%
I like lessons where I can make something				
Agree a lot	804	63.5%	563	55.8%
Agree..	362	28.6%	363	36.0%
Not sure	51	4.0%	30	2.9%
Disagree	24	1.9%	40	4.0%
Disagree a lot	18	1.4%	14	1.4%
Missing	6	.5%	–	–
I like lessons where we talk about our ideas				
Agree a lot	447	35.3%	313	31.0%
Agree..	525	41.5%	492	48.8%
Not sure	108	8.5%	72	7.1%
Disagree	125	9.9%	92	9.1%
Disagree a lot	55	4.3%	39	3.9%
Missing	5	.4%	1	.1%

For all these statements the primary school pupils were more likely to opt for the most positive response. However, when the two positive responses ('agree a lot' and 'agree') were combined, the differences between the two groups were either reversed (i.e. the proportion of pupils expressing a positive response was higher amongst the secondary pupils than amongst those in primary school) or became negligible.

3.4 Pupils' behaviour in school and out-of-school activities

In order to collect information about pupils' behaviour in school, their participation in extracurricular activities and their use of their leisure time, statements and questions were included in the pupils' questionnaires focusing on the areas of:

- pupils' perceptions of their ability and perseverance
- pupils' behaviour in school (including truancy and bullying)
- pupils' activities within and outside school.

3.4.1 Pupils' perceptions of their ability and perseverance

Pupils were asked to respond to two statements and two questions concerning their school work. Table 3.11 shows pupils' responses.

In terms of their effort within lessons, the majority of pupils at both age groups indicated that they worked as hard as they could in 'all' or 'most' lessons (a total of 85 per cent for top primary and 86 per cent for first-year secondary pupils).

When asked 'How good do you think you are at school work?', two-thirds of the primary pupils and three-quarters of the secondary pupils rated themselves 'about as good as most of my class'. The remaining pupils were fairly evenly split between those who perceived themselves as 'better than' and 'not as good as most of my class'.

When asked 'How do you think your teacher(s) would describe your school work?', the responses of the secondary pupils were virtually the same. The primary school pupils' responses, however, suggested that a small number of pupils who had rated themselves as 'better than' or 'not as good as most of the class' felt that their teachers would have described their work as 'about as good as most of the class'.

The responses to the statement 'I get good marks for my work' indicated that, in total, over half the primary pupils and nearly two-thirds of the secondary pupils received good marks for 'all' or 'most lessons' (52 per cent and 63 per cent respectively). The proportions of pupils who seldom, if ever, received good marks ('hardly any lessons' and 'no lessons') were small (eight per cent of primary pupils and three per cent of secondary).

Table 3.11 Perceptions of ability and perserverence: the responses of top primary and first-year secondary pupils compared

	primary		secondary	
Total.........	1265	100%	1009	100%
I work as hard as I can in school				
All lessons...	420	33.2%	305	30.2%
Most lessons	650	51.4%	565	56.0%
Some lessons...	177	14.0%	124	12.2%
Hardly any lessons	9	.7%	9	.9%
No lessons	4	.3%	4	.4%
Missing	5	.4%	2	.2%
How good do you think you are at school work?				
Better than most of my class	189	14.9%	142	14.1%
As good as most of my class	833	65.8%	746	73.9%
Not as good as most of my class	232	18.3%	112	11.1%
Missing	12	.9%	10	1.0%
I get good marks for my work				
All lessons...	87	6.9%	80	8.0%
Most lessons	575	45.5%	558	55.3%
Some lessons...	499	39.4%	338	33.5%
Hardly any lessons	81	6.4%	22	2.1%
No lessons	16	1.3%	9	.9%
Missing	6	.5%	3	.3%
How do you think your teacher(s) would describe your school work?				
Better than most of my class	154	12.2%	122	12.1%
As good as most of my class	948	74.9%	770	76.3%
Not as good as most of my class	149	11.8%	102	10.1%
Missing	13	1.0%	14	1.4%

3.4.2 Pupils' behaviour in school

For this aspect, two questions referred to general behaviour in school, two explored the issue of truancy and one statement raised the subject of bullying. Table 3.12 shows pupils' responses to the statements concerning general behaviour.

Table 3.12 Behaviour in school this year: the responses of top primary and first-year secondary pupils compared

	primary		secondary	
Total.........	1265	100%	1009	100%
Describe your behaviour in class and around school this year				
Always well behaved......................................	180	14.2%	152	15.0%
Usually well behaved	807	63.8%	662	65.6%
Sometimes badly behaved	240	19.0%	177	17.6%
Often badly behaved	30	2.4%	13	1.3%
Missing	7	.6%	5	.5%
How often have you had punishments this year?				
Never..	567	44.8%	421	41.7%
Once or twice...	574	45.3%	488	48.3%
Quite often	81	6.4%	63	6.3%
Often	35	2.7%	33	3.3%
Missing	9	.7%	4	.4%

Overall, the responses indicated that the majority of pupils saw themselves as generally well behaved: roughly eight out of ten pupils from each age group reported that they were 'always' or 'usually well behaved'. Fewer than three per cent of each age group acknowledged that they were 'often badly behaved'.

The responses to the question 'How often have you had punishments this year?' confirmed the picture portrayed in responses to the previous question. A sizeable number had 'never' had punishments during that school year (45 per cent of primary and 42 per cent of secondary), whilst similar proportions had only had punishments 'once or twice' (45 and 48 per cent respectively). The small number of pupils who admitted that they were 'quite often' or 'often' punished suggests that bad behaviour is not a major issue within top primary or first-year secondary classrooms.

Pupils were asked two questions on the subject of truancy: whether or not they had played truant that year, and, if they had, how often. Their responses to these two questions are combined in Table 3.13.

Fewer than ten per cent of pupils in each age group had played truant that year. Pupils from both age groups who played truant were most likely to skip a whole day (four per cent of both age groups). Smaller proportions of both groups reported missing 'one or two lessons, occasionally' (two per cent of primary and three per cent of secondary) and even smaller proportions 'days or weeks at a time'.

Table 3.13   Truancy: the responses of top primary and first-year secondary pupils compared

	primary		secondary	
Total.........	1265	100%	1009	100%
How often have you played truant this year?				
One or two lessons, occasionally	20	1.6%	34	3.4%
A whole day, occasionally.............................	55	4.4%	43	4.2%
Several days at a time	5	.4%	7	.6%
Weeks at a time...	10	.8%	5	.5%
I have not played truant	1167	92.3%	915	90.7%
Missing	8	.7%	5	.5%

The final question in this section asked about the frequency of bullying within the school; pupils' responses are shown in table 3.14.

Table 3.14   Bullying: the responses of top primary and first-year secondary pupils compared

	primary		secondary	
Total.........	1265	100%	1009	100%
Have you even been bullied in school this year?				
Never...	611	48.3%	444	44.0%
Once or twice..	450	35.5%	449	44.5%
Quite often	125	9.9%	77	7.6%
Often	72	5.7%	34	3.4%
Missing	7	.5%	5	.5%

Over half the pupils at each age group said they had been bullied in school that year – a disturbingly high proportion. Six per cent of the primary pupils reported that they were 'often' bullied (this equates to roughly one in 20 pupils, typically at least one pupil in an average class) and a further ten per cent that they were 'quite often' bullied. The proportions for the secondary pupils were slightly lower: three per cent reported being bullied 'often' and a further seven per cent 'quite often'. Although these responses seem to be rather worrying, it should be borne in mind that, apart from the wording of the question, no other definition of bullying was given to the samples of pupils; it is therefore possible that different pupils will have applied different definitions. However, if such a large number of pupils are affected by bullying of some description, it is surely an area worthy of further investigation and research.

3.4.3 Pupils' activities within and outside school

Pupils were asked about their participation in activities out of school hours, homework and a small number of activities that might occupy their leisure time. Their responses are shown in Tables 3.15 and 3.16.

Table 3.15   School-related activities: the responses of top primary and first-year secondary pupils compared

	primary		secondary	
Total.........	1265	100%	1009	100%
Do you take part in any lunch hour or after school activities?				
Yes	928	73.4%	631	62.6%
No...	219	17.3%	322	31.9%
There are no lunch hour or				
after school activities	112	8.9%	43	4.3%
Missing	5	.4%	13	1.3%
How many hours per day do you normally spend doing homework?				
I am not usually given homework	539	42.6%	28	2.7%
I am given homework but I don't do it	1	3.3%	23	2.2%
Half hour or less	304	24.0%	203	20.2%
About 1 hour	205	16.2%	395	39.1%
About 1 and a half hours	75	5.9%	196	19.4%
About 2 hours	36	2.9%	91	9.0%
About 2 and a half hours	17	1.3%	23	2.3%
3 hours or more	13	1.0%	20	2.0%
Missing	35	2.7%	32	3.1%
Homework is important in helping me to do well at school				
Agree a lot	589	46.5%	415	41.1%
Agree...	493	39.0%	447	44.3%
Not sure	114	9.0%	44	4.3%
Disagree	48	3.8%	80	8.0%
Disagree a lot	19	1.5%	23	2.3%
Missing	2	.1%	–	–

More top primary than first-year secondary pupils took part in extracurricular activities offered by their schools (73 per cent as compared with 63 per cent, despite the fact that almost one in ten primary schools did not organise out-of-hours activities). Almost one-third of the first-year secondary pupils surveyed did not participate in extracurricular activities, although virtually all secondary schools offered them. The responses from the Year 7 sample in the previous study were virtually the same as those reported here and even fewer Year 9 students participated in extracurricular activities (53 per cent). Taken overall, these responses suggest a diminishing interest in out-of-hours activities as pupils grow older; reasons for this are unclear, but might include increasing pressure as national tests/examinations approach, more time spent on homework, and/or increased peer pressure to pursue other leisure activities.

Not surprisingly, the responses concerning time spent on homework each day were very different for the two age groups. Roughly two out of five primary pupils (43 per cent) indicated that they were not usually given homework. Most of the primary pupils who **were** set homework spent half an hour or less doing it (24 per cent of all the primary sample) and about 16 per cent spent about an hour a day. Only about one in ten of the primary pupils spent an hour and a half or longer doing homework.

For the secondary school pupils the picture was rather different: virtually all indicated that they were given homework. The majority (nearly 60 per cent) spent one hour or one and a half hours doing homework each day. About 20 per cent spent less time (half an hour or less) and about 13 per cent spent more time (two hours or more). At both age groups, a small minority of pupils admitted that they were set homework, but did not do it (three per cent of primary and two per cent of secondary pupils).

Despite the fact that there was such a marked difference in homework allocation for the two age groups, there was a consensus of views in responding to the statement 'Homework is important in helping me to do well at school'. The majority of top primary and first-year secondary pupils agreed with the statement (86 per cent and 85 per cent respectively), although within those totals slightly more primary pupils chose to 'agree a lot' (47 per cent compared with 41 per cent of the secondary pupils).

The remaining questions in this section concerned the time allocated to three leisure activities: watching TV/videos, playing computer games and reading for fun. Pupils' responses are shown in Table 3.16.

Watching television and/or videos was clearly a very popular way for pupils to spend their leisure time, with about half of each age group spending about two or three hours each day in this way. Very few pupils indicated that they did not watch TV/videos, whereas, rather surprisingly, about one in ten pupils from each age group reported spending six hours or more each day watching TV/videos.

32

Table 3.16 Leisure activities: the responses of top primary and first-year secondary pupils compared

	primary		secondary	
Total.........	1265	100%	1009	100%
How often do you read on your own for fun outside school?				
(Almost) every day	577	45.6%	381	37.7%
Once or twice a week	357	28.3%	320	31.7%
Once or twice a month.................................	135	10.6%	154	15.2%
Never or hardly ever	184	14.5%	145	14.4%
Missing	12	1.0%	10	1.0%
How many hours each day do you watch television/videos?				
I don't watch television/videos	27	2.1%	17	1.7%
Up to 1 hour	251	19.8%	167	16.5%
About 2 hours	332	26.2%	257	25.5%
About 3 hours	278	22.0%	218	21.6%
About 4 hours	144	11.4%	62	16.1%
About 5 hours	78	6.1%	80	8.0%
6 hours or more	140	11.1%	94	9.3%
Missing	16	1.3%	14	1.3%
How many hours each day do you play computer games?				
I don't play computer games	269	21.2%	255	25.3%
Up to 1 hour	542	42.9%	437	43.3%
About 2 hours	199	15.7%	147	14.6%
About 3 hours	89	7.1%	75	7.4%
About 4 hours	50	3.9%	26	2.6%
About 5 hours	23	1.8%	11	1.1%
6 hours or more	61	4.8%	43	4.2%
Missing	32	2.6%	15	1.5%

Although the majority of pupils from both age groups indicated that they spent some time each day playing computer games, the time involved was not excessive: most spent up to one hour (43 per cent of both groups). About 20 per cent of the primary pupils, and a quarter of the secondary pupils reported that they did not play computer games; in some cases it is likely that this was simply because the pupils did not have access to computer games.

Whilst pupils are obviously spending significant amounts of their leisure time using modern technology (in the form of TV/videos and computer games), there is clearly still a place for reading for fun. Forty-six per cent of the top primary pupils and 38 per cent of the first-year secondary pupils reported reading for fun '(almost) every day'. A further three out of ten pupils at both age groups read for fun 'once or twice a week'. However, whilst these findings are generally encouraging, many people within the education sector will be concerned at the fact that 25 per cent of top primary pupils and 30 per cent of first-year secondary pupils only read for fun once or twice a month or less.

3.5 Parents' attitudes

There were a number of statements and questions in the questionnaire concerned with pupils' perceptions of their parents' attitudes to school and education. These fell into two main groups: those concerned with their parents' views on the value of education; and those concerned with parental interest and support.

3.5.1 Parents' views about the value of education

The pupils' responses to the statements relating to their perceptions of their parents' opinions about the value of education are shown in Table 3.17.

Table 3.17 Parents' opinions about the value of education: the responses of top primary and first-year secondary pupils compared

	primary		secondary	
Total.........	1265	100%	1009	100%
My parents think it is important for me to do well at school				
Agree a lot	1063	84.0%	850	84.2%
Agree..	176	13.9%	144	14.3%
Not sure	10	.8%	7	.7%
Disagree	8	.7%	2	.2%
Disagree a lot	5	.4%	2	.2%
Missing	3	.2%	3	.3%
My parents think school is a waste of time				
Agree a lot	10	.8%	7	.7%
Agree..	6	.5%	5	.5%
Not sure	40	3.2%	18	1.8%
Disagree	23	9.7%	105	10.4%
Disagree a lot	084	85.7%	874	86.6%
Missing	2	.2%	–	–

The majority of pupils in both age groups believed that their parents held positive opinions about the value of education and there were no significant differences between the responses of the primary and secondary pupils. For example, almost all (98 per cent) of both groups agreed or agreed a lot with the statement 'My parents think it is important for me to do well at school' and there were no differences between the proportions in each group agreeing a lot (84 per cent). Similar proportions disagreed or disagreed a lot with the statement 'My parents think school is a waste of time'.

3.5.2 Parental interest and support

The questionnaire contained a number of questions designed to obtain pupils' perceptions of parental interest and support. Their responses, which are shown in Table 3.18, suggest that, although the majority of parents demonstrate interest in their children's progress at school in a practical way, a minority do not.

Over 90 per cent of pupils in both age groups believed that their parents were 'always' or 'nearly always' interested in how they did at school, and very few (two per cent and one per cent) indicated that their parents 'never' or 'hardly ever' showed any interest. Further confirmation of parental interest is provided by the pupils' responses to the question on school parents' evenings: nearly 90 per cent of the primary pupils and 86 per cent of those in the secondary school said that their parents 'always' or 'nearly always' attended parents' evenings.

The majority of pupils believed that their parents were concerned that they should behave well in school. Over 90 per cent of pupils in both age groups said that their parents made it clear how they should behave in school and 87 per cent indicated their parents 'always' or 'nearly always' made sure they did their homework.

The secondary school pupils were also asked to say whether or not they thought their parents wanted them to remain in education after the age of 16: about 60 per cent thought that their parents wanted them to stay on and only seven per cent thought their parents wanted them to leave school as soon as possible. Just under a quarter were uncertain about their parents' views.

Table 3.18   Parents' interest and support: the responses of top primary and first-year secondary pupils compared

	primary		secondary	
Total.........	1265	100%	1009	100%
What do you think that your parents want you to do?				
Go into the sixth form of this school.............	NA	NA	377	37.3%
Go to another school or college....................	NA	NA	297	29.5%
Get a job as soon as possible........................	NA	NA	74	7.4%
Not sure..	NA	NA	233	23.1%
Missing	NA	NA	28	2.7%
My parents are interested in how I do at school				
Always	971	76.7%	797	79.0%
Nearly always	195	15.4%	145	14.4%
Sometimes..	76	6.0%	55	5.5%
Hardly ever	12	.9%	6	.6%
Never	9	.7%	1	.1%
Missing	2	.2%	4	.4%
My parents come to school parents' evenings				
Always	857	67.8%	633	62.7%
Nearly always	268	21.2%	236	23.4%
Sometimes..	99	7.8%	92	9.1%
Hardly ever	22	1.7%	23	2.2%
Never..	15	1.2%	22	2.2%
Missing	4	.3%	4	.4%
My parents make it clear that I should behave myself in school				
Agree a lot	701	55.4%	535	53.0%
Agree..	478	37.8%	413	40.9%
Not sure	48	3.8%	32	3.2%
Disagree	27	2.2%	26	2.5%
Disagree a lot	4	.3%	3	.3%
Missing	8	.6%	1	.1%
My parents make sure I do my homework				
Always	877	69.3%	683	67.7%
Nearly always	226	17.9%	195	19.4%
Sometimes..	95	7.5%	93	9.3%
Hardly ever	21	1.7%	18	1.8%
Never..	32	2.5%	16	1.6%
Missing	14	1.1%	3	.3%

3.6 The pupils' own post-16 intentions

3.6.1 Staying on

The pupils were asked whether or not they thought they would remain at school or college after the age of 16 (the end of year 11). Their responses are shown in Table 3.19.

Table 3.19 Post-16 intentions: the responses of top primary and first-year secondary pupils compared

	primary		secondary	
Total.........	1265	100%	1009	100%
After taking exams at the end of Year 11 do you expect to:				
go into the sixth form of this school/ your secondary school?	336	26.6%	304	30.2%
go to another school or college?	313	24.8%	292	29.0%
get a job as soon as possible?	178	14.1%	119	11.8%
Not sure?	429	33.9%	277	27.4%
Missing	9	.7%	16	1.6%

Not unexpectedly, a third of the top primary school pupils had not yet made up their minds. About a quarter expected to remain at their secondary school after the age of 16 and about a quarter thought they would go to another school or college. About 14 per cent said they intended to get a job as soon as possible. The responses of the secondary school pupils present a similar picture, although the proportion who had not made up their minds was slightly smaller (27 per cent) and the proportions opting for their own or another school slightly higher (about 30 per cent). About 12 per cent intended to leave school as soon as possible. Although it is likely that many of these pupils will change their minds as they get older, it may be of concern that more than 14 per cent of the 11-year-olds and 12 per cent of the 12-year-olds were intending to leave school at the earliest possible opportunity. It is interesting to note that the percentage of secondary school pupils intending to leave school as soon as possible was higher than the percentage who believed that their parents wanted them to leave (Table 3.18).

3.7 Pupils' comments

In the final question of the questionnaire, pupils were invited to comment on their schools in an open question 'Is there anything else, good or bad, you would like to write about your school?' A number of prompts were provided in order to help pupils to focus their thoughts. These prompts are shown below:

'You might want to write about
- how hard you find work at school
- how helpful teachers are when you're not sure about work
- what you like **best** about your school
- what you like **least** about your school
- bullying at school.'

Pupils' responses to this open-ended question were coded individually; the coding system was based on the range of responses found on examination of a sample of 100 questionnaires from each age group. Each sample was considered separately, so that the coding system devised would accurately reflect the range of responses made by that specific age group. However, there was a high level of agreement between the two samples, such that most of the categories of comments were common to both age groups, with only a small number which were specific to either top primary or first-year secondary pupils.

The categories of comments which were common to both year groups were:
- positive about school
- negative about school
- positive about teachers
- negative about teachers
- school work
- meals/lunchtimes
- bullying
- aspects liked best
- aspects liked least
- suggestions for changes/improvements
- other.

One further category was identified in the top primary sample:
- comments about the pupil's next school.

Two additional categories were identified in the secondary sample:
- comments about specific subjects
- personal goals/reflections.

Forty-three per cent of the primary school pupils and 59 per cent of the secondary pupils made comments about their school. Table 3.20 shows the responses; it should be remembered that the number of comments made on different aspects of school life (as identified above) varied from one pupil to another, since pupils were able to make several comments (a maximum of five comments per pupil were coded).

Table 3.20 Pupils' comments on their school: the responses of top primary and first-year secondary pupils compared

	primary		secondary	
Total.........	1265	100%	1009	100%
Positive about school	88	6.9%	91	9.0%
Negative about school......................................	32	2.5%	54	5.3%
Positive about teachers	244	19.3%	227	22.5%
Negative about teachers	57	4.5%	95	9.5%
School work	104	8.2%	146	14.4%
Next school	18	1.4%	NA	NA
Specific subjects	NA	NA	31	3.1%
Personal goals/reflections	NA	NA	31	3.1%
Meals/lunchtimes	11	.8%	14	1.4%
Bullying...	109	8.6%	156	15.5%
Aspects liked best	130	10.3%	134	13.3%
Aspects liked least	48	3.8%	75	7.4%
Suggestions for changes/improvements	23	1.8%	40	3.9%
Other..	1	.1%	15	1.5%
Pupils making no comment	719	57%	417	41%

NB Pupils could make up to five comments; totals do not sum to 100%.

The range of comments offered by pupils was particularly interesting. Not surprisingly, many related in some way to the prompts that were provided in the question (see above), such as the aspects of school liked best/least and comments concerning bullying. However, some of the categories identified were less obviously suggested by the prompts, for example pupils' personal goals and suggestions for changes/improvements.

Some of the responses provided by pupils under the categories identified are listed below (in general the comments from primary and secondary pupils were similar, but where a particular comment was specific to one group, this is shown in brackets):

- **Positive about school:** the school has many after-school activities, e.g. sports, plays; people are friendly and polite; will be sad to leave (primary); we don't have drugs in our school (secondary).

- **Negative about school:** dirty toilets; too much fighting; not enough things to do at break; too many rules; children put bubble gum under tables and chairs, despite the rule; too much smoking and pregnancy (secondary).

- **Positive about teachers:** teachers are very helpful; I like the teachers; teachers are caring/kind/friendly; teachers are willing to help whatever the situation; will miss the teachers (primary).

- **Negative about teachers:** teachers should listen more; teachers don't always help when you ask; should explain more clearly; some are very sarcastic; some teachers should be less sexist; wish teachers would mark work faster; teachers pay most attention to people who aren't much good at work.

- **School work:** I enjoy most lessons; work is just right; like finding out new things; work is sometimes hard, sometimes easy; homework is bad because evenings are our own time (secondary); too much work for holidays (secondary).

- **Next school** (primary only): not many children going to my next school, but I'll make friends; looking forward to next school; will miss friends when I move to next school.

- **Specific subjects** (secondary only): maths is difficult; hard maths work; maths work is too easy; French I don't take much interest because I don't know what to do.

- **Personal goals/reflections** (secondary only): teachers help but sometimes I just don't understand; want to do better at reading; want to help keep school clean and try to stop bullying; not very good at geography.

- **Meals/lunchtimes:** don't like dinner ladies; not allowed pop for a packed lunch; drinking water is warm; should be allowed to bring bottled water; have to wait to go in for dinner; better things to eat in canteen (secondary).

- **Bullying:** never been bullied; there aren't many bullies in school; bullies are expelled; teachers are good at controlling bullying; I get bullied a lot; I used to get picked on but not any more; a girl in my class has been bullied – it should be stopped.

- **Aspects liked best:** people are friendly; lunchtimes are best at school; maths; English; creative lessons in school especially art; PE; subjects that will help me become a vet; school has a good science department (secondary); like using computers; where we do things (primary); reading; most lessons; like teachers and subjects best.

- **Aspects liked least:** other children think you're stupid; don't like 3.15 p.m.; hate spelling; hate games; children telling stories about each other; assemblies; English; music; French; detentions; the school is dirty; when it's cold teachers still make children go outside; fund-raising for school; sharing books.

- **Suggestions for changes/improvements:** need more facilities for wet play; better equipment; should change morning hours to start later; should do more exercise; should be able to go to the toilet when we want; would be better if school were co-educational; should be more notice of after school activities; want basketball practice for first-years (secondary); would like more concerts.

The 'Other' category included all comments (including irrelevant ones) that did not fall into the above categories, such as 'No comment' and 'I can't think of anything'.

Clearly, pupils in both age groups commented on aspects of school life that were important to them: some pupils' comments focused on academic aspects, such as the subjects they liked/disliked, whereas for others opportunities to participate in games and sports seemed a high priority. One secondary pupil seemed concerned that his efforts were unrecognised by his teachers, leading him to comment: 'Teachers don't give me commendations when I deserve them.' For another secondary pupil, the subject of school meals was an area of both celebration and frustration: having commented that the meals were better than at his primary school, he went on to complain: 'But the school keeps changing the size of our chips. I like thin French fries best.'

Leaving individual remarks aside, it is evident that the category that accounted for the highest number of comments from both primary and secondary pupils concerned positive comments about teachers (19 per cent and 23 per cent respectively). At each age group, far fewer negative comments were made about teachers (five per cent for primary and ten per cent for secondary).

The other areas that attracted relatively high number of comments from both age groups were school work, bullying and aspects of school liked best. Interestingly, rather more secondary than primary pupils referred to school work and bullying; reasons for this are not clear.

In general, the pattern of pupils' responses when they were asked to give their own comments was encouraging: the positive remarks outnumbered the negative ones and suggested that, overall, most pupils were contented in their school life.

3.8 Summary

Attitudes towards school and learning

♦ The findings reported in this chapter suggest that the majority find school a positive experience.

♦ The study identified a worrying minority – about ten per cent of pupils – who are disaffected in their attitudes towards school. The size of this minority was slightly larger amongst the first-year secondary pupils than amongst those in the primary school (Table 3.1).

♦ Top primary pupils tended to hold slightly more positive attitudes towards school than did pupils in the first year of secondary school.

♦ The majority of pupils believed that schools had an important role to play in terms of preparing them for examinations and the world of work (Table 3.4).

♦ The majority of pupils in both age groups believed that their school was well regarded. Primary school pupils, however, were more likely to agree with the statement 'My school is clean and tidy' (Table 3.5).

Teachers, teaching and discipline

♦ Primary school pupils were far more likely than those in the secondary school to say that they liked their teachers (Table 3.6).

♦ The majority of pupils in both age groups reported that their teachers monitored their work regularly, encouraged them to work hard, took action when they saw anyone breaking the rules and made it clear how pupils should behave in school (Tables 3.7 and 3.8). There were very few differences between the responses of the primary and secondary pupils.

♦ The primary school pupils were more likely than those in the secondary school to agree that their teachers could keep order in class (Table 3.8).

♦ The secondary school pupils were more likely to think that their school had too many rules and the primary school pupils more likely to agree that their school had sensible rules (Table 3.8).

♦ About half of the pupils in both age groups said that they never had individual discussions with their class teacher about their work during the current school year and a similar proportion of secondary pupils said they had never had a one-to-one discussion about their work with other teachers (Table 3.9).

♦ The two most popular types of lessons with both age groups were those where pupils could work with their friends or those where they could make something (Table 3.10).

Self-reported ability and behaviour

♦ The majority of pupils in both age groups said that they worked as hard as they could in all/most lessons; there were no differences between the two age groups. The secondary school pupils, however, were slightly more likely to think they were good at school work and to say that they obtained good marks in all/most lessons (Table 3.11).

♦ The majority of pupils considered that they were well behaved in school and there were very few differences in the perceptions of the two age groups (Table 3.12).

♦ Fewer than ten per cent of pupils in each age group had played truant during the current school year (Table 3.13).

♦ Over half of the pupils in each age group said that they had been bullied during the current school year; in most cases this had been once or twice although 16 per cent of primary school pupils and 11 per cent of primary school pupils indicated that they had been bullied often or quite often (Table 3.14).

Out-of-school activities

♦ Top primary pupils were more likely than those in the secondary school to take part in extracurricular activities offered by the schools (Table 3.15).

♦ The majority of pupils in both age groups agreed that homework was important in helping them to do well in school. Not unexpectedly, the secondary school pupils spent more time on homework than those in the primary school, about 40 per cent of whom said they were not usually given homework (Table 3.15).

♦ Primary school pupils spent more time than those in the secondary school reading for pleasure outside school, possibly because they spent less time on homework. Nearly half of the primary school pupils and about a third of the secondary school pupils said that they read for fun (almost) every day (Table 3.16).

♦ Almost all of the pupils spent some time watching TV/videos each day. The majority (about two-thirds of each age group) spent up to three hours watching TV/videos each day (Table 3.16). However, a minority (about one in ten of each age group) said they spent six hours or more each day.

♦ About three-quarters of the pupils in both age groups spent some time each day playing computer games (Table 3.16). However, the time involved was not normally excessive: 43 per cent of both groups spent up to an hour each day.

Parents' attitudes

♦ The majority of pupils in both age groups believed that their parents held positive opinions about the value of education, were interested in how their children performed at school and encouraged them to work hard and behave well (Tables 3.17 and 3.18). There were few differences between the responses of the two age groups.

Pupils' comments on schools

♦ In the pupils' responses to the question 'Is there anything else, good or bad, you would like to write about your school?' (Table 3.20), positive comments outnumbered negative ones. Positive comments about their teachers were made by about 20 per cent of the pupils in both age groups; teachers were described as helpful, caring, kind and friendly. Pupils made far fewer negative comments about teachers. Other topics which attracted relatively high numbers of comments from both age groups were school work, bullying and aspects of school liked best.

CHAPTER 4

DIFFERENCES BETWEEN THE RESPONSES OF BOYS AND GIRLS

4.1 Introduction

The purposes of this chapter are to identify any differences between the attitudes towards school and education of girls and boys, and to compare the size of each gender difference found amongst top primary school children with the size of the corresponding gender difference amongst the first-year secondary pupils taking part in this study.

The material in this chapter is ordered in the same way as in Chapter 3. Girls' and boys' attitudes have therefore been compared under the following main headings:

♦ attitudes towards school and learning

♦ teachers, teaching and discipline

♦ self-reported ability and behaviour

♦ perceptions of parental interest and home support.

Comparisons between girls and boys have normally been made in terms of the combined percentages selecting the two positive options ('agree a lot' and 'agree'). Where appropriate, differences between the percentages selecting the most positive option ('agree a lot') have been highlighted. The chi-square test has been used to determine the statistical significance of any differences between the two samples. As in the previous chapter, the five per cent level of statistical significance has been accepted as evidence of difference between the two groups. In the description which follows, the girls' responses have been described first, and statistically significant differences between girls and boys have been highlighted by bullet points.

The figures in this chapter are designed to show whether there were any statistically significant differences between the responses of girls and boys and, if there were, which sex was more likely to opt for what we considered to be the most positive response. Full details of the proportions of boys and girls opting for each response are given in Tables 4.1 to 4.20 in Section 4.8 at the end of this chapter.

4.2 Attitudes towards school and learning

4.2.1 Like and dislike of school

The directions of any differences between the girls' and boys' responses to the three statements concerned with like and dislike of school are shown in Figure 4.1.

Figure 4.1   Like and dislike of school: differences between the responses of girls and boys

STATEMENT	Gender more likely to select the positive response in:	
	Top primary	First-year secondary
I am very happy when I am at school	😊	😊
On the whole I like being at school	😊	😊
Most of the time I don't want to go to school	😊	=

 Girls more likely to have a more positive attitude (difference statistically significant)

= *No difference*

 Boys more likely to have a more positive attitude (difference statistically significant)

Our findings show that girls in top primary *and* first-year secondary classes are *more likely* than boys to express positive attitudes towards school (Figure 4.1 and Table 4.1). For example:

- The girls were *more likely* than the boys to 'agree a lot' or 'agree' with the statement 'I am very happy when I am at school' (77 per cent compared with 70 per cent in top primary classes; and 76 per cent compared with 68 per cent in first-year secondary classes). The size of the gender difference is similar in both sectors.

- The girls were *more likely* than the boys to agree a lot with the statement 'On the whole I like being at school' (33 per cent compared with 28 per cent in the primary school; and 28 per cent compared with 17 per cent in the secondary school). The magnitude of the gender difference was greater amongst the first-year secondary school pupils (11 percentage points) than amongst those at the top of the primary school (five percentage points).

- The girls in the primary schools were *less likely* than the boys to 'agree a lot' or 'agree' with the statement 'Most of the time I don't want to go to school' (24 per cent compared with 35 per cent, a difference of 11 percentage points). In the secondary schools, however, the difference between the girls' and boys' responses was smaller (34 per cent compared with 38 per cent) and not statistically significant.

4.2.2 Interest or boredom in lessons

The directions of any differences between the girls' and boys' responses to the three statements concerned with interest or boredom in lessons are shown in Figure 4.2 and Table 4.2.

Figure 4.2   Interest and boredom in lessons: differences between the responses of girls and boys

STATEMENT	Gender more likely to select the positive response in:	
	Top primary	First-year secondary
The work I do in lessons is interesting to me	=	=
I am bored in lessons	☺	=
In a lesson I often count the minutes till breaktime	☺	☺

In general, the gender differences in favour of girls were slightly smaller for this set of statements than they were for those concerned with liking for school. There were no differences between the responses of boys and girls in either age group to the statement 'The work I do in lessons is interesting to me' or, amongst the first-year secondary pupils, to the statement 'I am bored in lessons'. However:

● At both top primary and first-year secondary levels, the girls were *less likely* than the boys to say that they counted the minutes to the end in all/ most lessons (24 per cent compared with 38 per cent at the top primary level; and 19 per cent compared with 24 per cent at the first-year secondary level).

● At the top primary level girls were *less likely* than boys to say they were bored in lessons (58 per cent compared with 42 per cent indicated that they were 'never' or 'hardly ever' bored in lessons). However, as stated above, there were no differences between the responses of the secondary girls and boys to this statement.

4.2.3 The value of school and school work

The directions of any differences between the girls' and boys' responses to the three statements concerned with the value of school and school work are shown in Figure 4.3 and Table 4.3.

Figure 4.3 **The value of school and school work: differences between the responses of girls and boys.**

STATEMENT	Gender more likely to select the positive response in:	
	Top primary	First-year secondary
School work is worth doing	(girl)	=
The work I do in lessons is a waste of time	(girl)	=
School is a waste of time for me	(girl)	=

● The study found that girls at the top primary level were more likely than boys to express positive attitudes towards the value of school work.

At the first-year secondary level, on the other hand, no statistically significant differences were found between the responses of boys and girls.

4.2.4 Pupils' perceptions of the purposes of school

The directions of any differences between the girls' and boys' responses to the three statements concerned with the purposes of schools are shown in Figure 4.4 and Table 4.4.

Figure 4.4 **Pupils' perceptions of the purposes of school: differences between the responses of girls and boys**

STATEMENT	Gender more likely to select the positive response in:	
	Top primary	First-year secondary
Schools should help us to do as well as possible in tests and exams (like GCSE)	(girl)	=
Schools should teach things that will be useful when we get jobs	=	=
Schools should help us to be independent and stand on our own two feet	=	=
Schools should help us to learn how to use our leisure time	(boy)	(boy)
School work doesn't help you get a job	=	=

As stated in the previous chapter, the majority of pupils believed that schools should help them to pass exams, get jobs and become independent and there were few differences in the strength of the girls' and boys' responses. However:

- The girls, at top primary and first-year secondary level, were slightly *less likely* to 'agree a lot' that schools should help them to learn how to use their leisure time (18 per cent of the primary school girls, compared with 24 per cent of the boys, agreed 'a lot' with this statement; 13 per cent of the secondary girls, compared with 18 per cent of the boys, agreed 'a lot');

- At primary level only, the girls were *more likely* than the boys to 'agree a lot' with the statement 'Schools should help us to do as well as possible in tests and exams' (70 per cent compared with 63 per cent of the boys). There were no differences between the responses of girls and boys at the first-year secondary level.

4.2.5 Perceived reputation of their school

The directions of any differences between the girls' and boys' responses to the two statements concerned with pupils' perceptions of the reputation of their school are shown in Figure 4.5 and Table 4.5.

Figure 4.5 Perceived reputation of their school: differences between the responses of girls and boys

STATEMENT	Gender more likely to select the positive response in:	
	Top primary	First-year secondary
People think this is a good school	☺ (girl)	=
My school is clean and tidy	☺ (girl)	☺ (girl)

In general, the girls were more likely to respond positively to these statements and the differences between boys and girls tended to be greater at the top primary than at the first-year secondary level.

- The primary and secondary school girls were *more likely* than the boys to *perceive* their school as 'always' or 'nearly always' clean and tidy (89 per cent of the primary school girls compared with 78 per cent of the boys; 74 per cent of the secondary girls compared with 64 per cent of the boys).

- Within the primary schools, the girls were more likely than the boys to 'agree a lot' or 'agree' with the statement 'People think this is a good school' (85 per cent compared with 81 per cent). There were no differences between the responses of the secondary school girls and boys.

4.3. Teachers, teaching and discipline

4.3.1 Liking for teachers

The direction of any differences between the girls' and boys' responses to the statement 'I like my teacher(s)' is shown in Figure 4.6 and Table 4.6.

Figure 4.6   Liking for teachers: differences between the responses of girls and boys

STATEMENT	Gender more likely to select the positive response in:	
	Top primary	First-year secondary
I like my teachers	☺	☺

- At the top primary and first-year secondary level, the girls were more likely than the boys to say that they 'always' liked their teacher(s) (49 per cent of the primary school girls compared with 37 per cent of the boys; 18 per cent of the secondary school girls, compared with 13 per cent of the boys).

As noted in Chapter 3, the large difference in the proportions of primary and secondary school pupils saying that they always liked their teacher(s) can probably be explained by the fact that the primary school pupils were thinking about one teacher (their class teacher) whereas the secondary school pupils were thinking about all the teachers who taught them.

4.3.2 Ensuring the quality of pupils' work

The directions of any differences between the girls' and boys' responses to the four statements relating to the strategies their teachers used to ensure the quality of pupils' work are shown in Figure 4.7 and Table 4.7.

In general, there were few differences between the responses of girls and boys to this set of statements. The majority of the girls and boys at both levels perceived their teachers as trying hard to encourage high quality work (see Section 3.3.2). Only one statistically significant difference was found:

- The upper primary girls were *more likely* than the boys to agree that their teacher 'always' marked their work (59 per cent compared with 55 per cent). There were no differences between the responses of the girls and boys at the first-year secondary level.

Figure 4.7 Ensuring the quality of pupils' work: differences between the responses of girls and boys

STATEMENT	Gender more likely to select the positive response in:	
	Top primary	First-year secondary
My teacher(s) always/usually/hardly ever marks my work	☺	=
My teacher(s) makes sure we do any homework that is set	=	=
My teacher(s) tries hard to make me work as well as I am able/are fairly easily satisfied/ don't seem to care whether I work or not	=	=
My teacher(s) tells me when I do my work well	=	=

4.3.3 Maintaining discipline

The directions of any differences between the girls' and boys' responses to the statement focusing on maintaining discipline within and outside the classroom are shown in Figure 4.8 and Table 4.8.

Figure 4.8 Maintaining discipline: differences between the responses of girls and boys

STATEMENT	Gender more likely to select the positive response in:	
	Top primary	First-year secondary
The teachers in my school take action when they see anyone breaking school rules	=	=
My teachers make it clear how we should behave in school	=	=
My teachers can control the class	☺	=
My school has sensible rules	=	☺
Discipline in school about right	=	=
No. of rules about right (boys say too many)	☺	☺

51

There were very few differences between the responses of girls and boys to this set of statements. The majority of boys and girls in both age groups expressed positive attitudes towards the way teachers maintained discipline in their schools. However:

- At the top primary and first-year secondary level, the girls were more likely than the boys to say that the number of rules in their school was 'about right' (83 per cent compared with 75 per cent of the boys at the top primary level; 75 per cent compared with 67 per cent of the boys at the first-year secondary level).

- On the other hand, the girls at the first-year secondary level were less likely than the boys to 'agree a lot' with the statement 'My school has sensible rules' (24 per cent compared with 30 per cent of the boys). It is possible, however, that this apparent contradiction can be explained by the fact that rules concerned with school uniform tend to be particularly disliked by secondary-school girls.

4.3.4 Talking individually to teachers

Figure 4.9 and Table 4.9 show that there were no differences between the girls' and boys' responses to the statements concerned with talking to teachers about their school work.

Figure 4.9   Talking individually to their teachers: differences between the responses of girls and boys

	Gender more likely to select the positive response in:	
STATEMENT	Top primary	First-year secondary
How often have you talked to your class teacher about your school work?	=	=
How often have you talked to other teachers about your school work?	NA	=

4.3.5 Types of lessons liked

The directions of any differences between the responses of girls and boys to statements concerned with the types of lessons liked are shown in Figure 4.10 and Table 4.10.

Figure 4.10   Types of lessons liked: differences between the responses of girls and boys

STATEMENT	Gender more likely to select the positive response in:	
	Top primary	First-year secondary
I like lessons where I can work with my friends	☺	=
I like lessons where I can work on my own	☺	=
I like lessons where I can make something	☺	☺
I like lessons where we talk about our ideas	=	=

The majority of pupils in both age groups agreed that they liked lessons where they could work with their friends, lessons in which they had discussions and lessons in which they could make something (see Chapter 3). They were less keen on lessons where they could work on their own. However, there were a few statistically significant differences between the responses of girls and boys.

- The top primary and first-year secondary girls were *less likely* than the boys to 'strongly agree' with the statement 'I like lessons where I can make something' (58 per cent compared with 69 per cent of the boys at the primary level; 50 per cent compared with 62 per cent of the boys at the first-year secondary level).

- Girls at the top primary level were *more likely* than the boys to 'agree a lot' that they liked lessons where they could work on their own (21 per cent compared with 16 per cent of the boys). There were no differences between the girls' and boys' responses at the first-year secondary level.

- Girls at the top primary level were *slightly less likely* to 'agree a lot' with the statement 'I like lessons where I can work with my friends' (63 per cent compared with 69 per cent of the boys). There were no differences between the responses of girls and boys at the first-year secondary level.

4.4. Self-reported ability and behaviour

4.4.1 Pupils' perceptions of their ability and perseverance

The directions of any differences between the girls' and boys' responses to the statement concerned with their perceptions of their own ability and perseverance are shown in Figure 4.11 and Table 4.11.

Figure 4.11   **Perceptions of ability and perseverance: differences between the responses of girls and boys**

STATEMENT	Gender more likely to select the positive response in:	
	Top primary	First-year secondary
I work as hard as I can in school	(girl)	(girl)
Pupils' perception of how good s/he is at school work	(boy)	=
I get good marks for my work	=	=
Pupils' perception of how good teachers think s/he is at school work	=	=

There were no statistically significant differences between the responses of the boys and girls in either age group in terms of their responses to the statement 'I get good marks for my work', or in terms of their perceptions of their teachers' estimation of their ability. However:

- Girls at the top primary and first-year secondary levels were more likely to say that they worked as hard as they could in all/most lessons (91 per cent of the top primary girls compared with 79 per cent of the boys; 89 per cent of the first-year secondary school girls compared with 84 per cent of the boys. The difference was larger at the primary level (12 percentage points compared with five percentage points at the first-year secondary level).

- The top primary girls were *more likely* than the boys to rate their ability at school work as 'as good as most of my class' (72 per cent of the girls compared with 60 per cent of the boys). Interestingly, the girls were *less likely* to rate themselves as better than most of their class (13 per cent compared with 17 per cent of the boys) *and* not as good as most of their class (15 per cent compared with 22 per cent). There were no differences in the responses of the girls and boys at the first-year secondary level.

4.4.2 Behaviour in school

The directions of any differences between the girls' and boys' responses to the statements focusing on their behaviour in school are shown in Figure 4.12 and Table 4.12.

The girls in both age groups tended to see themselves as better behaved than the boys and fewer had received punishments, such as lines, being kept in, or having detentions during the school year of the survey.

Figure 4.12   Behaviour in school this year: differences between the responses of girls and boys

STATEMENT	Gender more likely to select the positive response in:	
	Top primary	First-year secondary
How would you describe your behaviour in class and around school this year?	😊	😊
How often have you had punishments, such as lines, detention, being kept in, etc. this year? (*girls less often*)	😊	😊

Our comparisons show that:

● The top primary and first-year secondary girls were *more likely* than the boys to say that they were always or usually well-behaved (86 per cent of the primary girls compared with 70 per cent of the boys; 86 per cent of the secondary girls compared with 75 per cent of the boys).

● The girls were also more *likely* to say that they had *never* received any punishments during the current school year (59 per cent of the primary girls compared with 30 per cent of the boys; 54 per cent of the secondary girls compared with 29 per cent of the boys).

4.4.3 Truancy and bullying

The directions of any differences between the girls' and boys' responses to the questions on truancy and bullying are shown in Figure 4.13 and Tables 4.13 and 4.14.

Our comparisons show that:

● The girls at the top primary and first-year secondary level were *less likely* than the boys to have played truant (six per cent compared with nine per cent of the boys at the primary level; six per cent compared with 12 per cent of the boys at the first-year secondary level).

Figure 4.13. Truancy and bullying: differences between the responses of girls and boys

STATEMENT	Gender more likely to select the positive response in:	
	Top primary	First-year secondary
Have you ever played truant this year? (*girls truant less*) Have you ever been bullied this year?	☺	☺
	=	=

As Figure 4.13 shows, there were no statistically significant differences between the responses of girls and boys with regard to having been bullied.

4.4.4 School-related activities

The directions of any differences between the girls' and boys' responses to the questions on school-related activities are shown in Figure 4.14 and Table 4.15.

Figure 4.14 School-related activities: differences between the responses of girls and boys

STATEMENT	Gender more likely to select the positive response in:	
	Top primary	First-year secondary
Participation in lunch hour/after school activities	=	☺
How many hours each day do you normally spend doing homework? (*girls spend more time*)	☺	☺
Homework is important in helping me to do well at school	☺	=

- *Fewer* of the secondary girls (59 per cent, compared with 66 per cent of the boys) reported taking part in such activities. There were no differences between the responses of the girls and boys at the top primary level.

- The girls at the top primary and first-year secondary level tended to *spend longer doing homework* than the boys. The difference was more marked at the first-year secondary level where 38 per cent of the girls, but only 27 per cent of the boys, spent one and a half hours or more each day on homework.

- Although the majority of the girls and boys in both age groups 'strongly agreed' or 'agreed' with the statement that homework was important in helping them to do well at school, the percentages were slightly higher for the girls at the primary level (87 per cent compared with 84 per cent). There were no differences between the responses of girls and boys at the first-year secondary level.

4.4.5 Out-of-school activities

The directions of the differences between the girls' and boys' responses to questions relating to leisure activities are shown in Figure 4.15 and Table 4.16.

Figure 4.15   Leisure activities: differences between the responses of girls and boys

STATEMENT	Gender more likely to select the positive response in:	
	Top primary	First-year secondary
How often do you read for fun outside school? (*girls spend more time*)	(girl)	(girl)
How many hours each day do you watch TV or videos? (*boys spend more time*)	(boy)	=
How many hours each day do you play computer games? (*boys spend more time*)	(boy)	(boy)

Our comparisons suggest that girls tend to spend much more time out of school reading for pleasure, whereas boys spend more time playing computer games and, to a lesser extent, watching TV and videos.

● The girls at the top primary and first-year secondary level were *much more likely* than the boys to report *reading for pleasure outside school (almost) every day* (57 per cent compared with 34 per cent of the boys at the primary level; 47 per cent compared with 28 per cent of the boys at the secondary level).

● The top primary girls reported *spending less time watching television or videos* than the boys (26 per cent, compared with 32 per cent of the boys, said they spent four hours or more watching TV or videos each day). There were no differences between the responses of the girls and boys at the first-year secondary level.

● The top primary and first-year secondary girls were *less likely than the boys to play computer games* (66 per cent of the top primary girls compared with 86 per cent of the boys, played computer games; 62 per cent of the secondary girls, compared with 84 per cent of the boys, played computer games each day).

4.5 Parents' attitudes

There were a number of statements and questions in the questionnaire concerned with pupils' perceptions of their parents' attitudes to school and education. These fell into two main groups: those concerned with their parents' views on the value of education; and those concerned with parental interest and support.

4.5.1 Parents' views about the value of education

The directions of any differences between the responses of girls and boys to the statements relating to the pupils' perceptions of their parents' opinions about the value of education are shown in Figure 4.16 and Table 4.17.

Figure 4.16   Parents' opinions about the value of education: differences between the responses of boys and girls

STATEMENT	Gender more likely to select the positive response in:	
	Top primary	First-year secondary
My parents think it is important for me to do well at school	=	=
My parents think school is a waste of time	😊	=

As Chapter 3 shows, the majority of pupils in both age groups believed that their parents held positive opinions about the value of education and there were few differences between the girls' and boys' responses. For example, there were no differences between the responses of boys and girls to the statement 'My parents think it is important for me to do well at school'. However:

● The top primary girls were slightly more likely than the boys to 'disagree a lot' with the statement 'My parents think school is a waste of time' (89 per cent compared with 83 per cent). There were no differences between the responses of the secondary girls and boys to this statement.

4.5.2 Parental interest and support

The directions of any differences between the responses of boys and girls to the questions and statements concerned with parental interest and support are shown in Figure 4.17 and Table 4.18.

There was only one difference between the responses of the girls and boys to this set of questions and statements.

Figure 4.17 Perceptions of parental interest and support: differences between the responses of girls and boys

STATEMENT	Gender more likely to select the positive response in:	
	Top primary	First-year secondary
Parents want child to stay on in education after 16 (*more boys thought their parents wanted them to get a job as soon as possible*)	NA	☺
My parents are interested in how I do at school	=	=
My parents come to school parents' evenings	=	=
My parents make it clear that I should behave well at school	=	=
My parents make sure I do my homework	=	=

- The first-year secondary school girls were less likely than the boys to believe that their parents wanted them to leave school and get a job as soon as possible (four per cent of the girls compared with 11 per cent of the boys). It is interesting to note that this difference is reflected in the pupils' own views (see below).

4.6 The pupils' own post-16 intentions

The directions of the differences between girls' and boys' responses to the question concerned with their post-16 intentions are shown in Figure 4.18 and Table 4.19.

Figure 4.18 Post-16 intentions: differences between the responses of girls and boys

STATEMENT	Gender more likely to select the positive response in:	
	Top primary	First-year secondary
Expect to stay in education after taking GCSE	☺	☺

- The girls, at the top primary and first-year secondary level, were more likely than the boys to intend to remain in education and *less likely* to intend to leave school as soon as possible (nine per cent of the top primary girls compared with 19 per cent of the boys and six per cent of the first-year secondary girls compared with 18 per cent of the boys intended to leave school as soon as possible).

The pupils were asked whether they had decided what job or career they would like to have when they left school. Those who had decided were asked to give the name of the job or career. About two-thirds of the top primary school pupils and 70 per cent of those in the first year of secondary school said they had already decided what they wanted to do.

The jobs most frequently selected by girls were:
- teacher (13 per cent of primary and 12 per cent of secondary);
- hairdresser/beautician (12 per cent of both age groups);
- working with animals (nine per cent of primary and 12 per cent of secondary);
- lawyer (six per cent and seven per cent);
- nurse (six per cent of both age groups);
- doctor (four per cent of both age groups);
- nursery nurse (two per cent of primary and six per cent of secondary);
- actress
- air hostess ⎤ (each selected by about four per cent of both age groups).
- artist. ⎦

The jobs most frequently mentioned by boys were:
- footballer (21 per cent and 18 per cent);
- the police force (seven per cent and four per cent);
- RAF or Navy pilot (five per cent and three per cent);
- airline pilot
- chef/baker
- doctor ⎤ (each selected by about three per cent
- fireman ⎦ of both age groups).
- mechanic
- working with computers.

Clearly, many of the pupils will change their minds as they grow older and become more realistic. For example, the job most frequently mentioned by boys was 'footballer'. It seems likely that most of these boys will opt for more realistic jobs as they become more mature.

4.7. Summary

Attitudes towards school and learning

♦ In both age groups, the girls were more likely than the boys to say that they liked school (Figure 4.1).

♦ The girls were slightly less likely to admit to boredom in lessons, but there were no differences in the girls' and boys' ratings of school work in terms of interest (Figure 4.2).

♦ At the top primary level, the girls held more positive attitudes than the boys towards the value of school and school work, but these differences were not found at the first-year secondary level (Figure 4.3).

♦ The majority of pupils of both sexes thought that schools should help them to do as well as possible (in tests and public exams), teach them things that would be useful to them when they got jobs and help them to become independent. They also believed that school work would help them to get a job. Boys, however, were slightly more likely to agree that schools should help them to learn how to use their leisure time (Figure 4.4).

♦ There were no gender differences between the girls and boys in terms of their response to the statement 'People think this is a good school'; the majority of pupils agreed with the statement. However, the girls in both age groups were more likely to say that their schools were clean and tidy. There is no obvious explanation for this (Figure 4.5).

Teachers, teaching and discipline

♦ The girls were more likely to say that they liked their teachers, but there were few differences between the girls' and boys' perceptions of the ways their teachers tried to ensure the quality of their work, or of their teachers' effectiveness in maintaining discipline (Figures 4.6 and 4.7).

Self-reported ability and behaviour

♦ The girls were more likely to be well-behaved, less likely to have received punishments such as lines or detentions, and more likely to say that they worked hard at school (Figures 4.11 and 4.12).

♦ The girls were less likely to say that they had played truant, but there were no differences between the proportions of the boys and girls being bullied (Figure 4.13).

♦ Although the top primary girls had very slightly lower perceptions of their own ability than the top primary boys, no difference was found at the first-year secondary level. There were no differences between the girls and boys in terms of how they thought their teachers rated their ability (Figure 4.11).

Out-of-school activities

♦ The girls tended to spend more time than the boys each day on homework, more time reading for pleasure, less time watching TV and videos. Boys were more likely to play computer games (Figure 4.15).

Perceptions of parents' attitudes

♦ There were very few differences between the girls' and boys' perceptions of parental support for their education, but slightly more of the boys believed that their parents wanted them to leave school as soon as possible. This was reflected in the pupils' own reported intentions (Figures 4.16 to 4.18). It should, however, be borne in mind that the proportions intending to leave school at the earliest possible opportunity were relatively small (19 per cent of the top primary boys and nine per cent of the girls, compared with 18 per cent of the first-year secondary boys and six per cent of the girls).

Future careers

♦ About two-thirds of the top primary school pupils and 70 per cent of the first-year secondary school pupils said they had already decided on their future career. The most popular jobs with girls were teacher, hairdresser/beautician, working with animals, lawyer, nurse and doctor. The most popular jobs with boys were: footballer, the police force, and RAF/Navy pilot.

4.8 Tables comparing the responses of boys and girls

Table 4.1 Likes and dislike of school: the responses of boys and girls compared

	Primary				Secondary			
	Boys		**Girls**		**Boys**		**Girls**	
Total	628	100%	635	100%	495	100%	508	100%
I am very happy when I am at school								
Agree a lot	85	13.5%	128	20.2%	48	9.7%	73	14.5%
Agree	355	56.5%	359	56.5%	289	58.5%	311	61.2%
Not sure	131	20.8%	111	17.5%	87	17.6%	65	12.7%
Disagree	42	6.8%	26	4.1%	55	11.1%	44	8.7%
Disagree a lot	12	2.0%	9	1.3%	15	3.1%	13	2.6%
Missing	3	.5%	2	.4%	–	–	1	.2%
On the whole I like being at school								
Agree a lot	174	27.7%	208	32.7%	84	17.0%	143	28.1%
Agree	331	52.8%	314	49.4%	318	64.3%	279	54.9%
Not sure	62	9.9%	78	12.3%	40	8.0%	39	7.8%
Disagree	44	7.0%	24	3.8%	39	7.8%	22	4.4%
Disagree a lot	15	2.4%	11	1.8%	13	2.7%	23	4.6%
Missing	2	.3%	–	–	1	.2%	1	.2%
Most of the time I don't want to go to school								
Agree a lot	76	12.1%	47	7.3%	60	12.0%	38	7.6%
Agree	142	22.7%	103	16.2%	130	26.3%	133	26.2%
Not sure	64	10.2%	88	13.8%	49	9.9%	42	8.3%
Disagree	212	33.8%	240	37.7%	178	35.9%	193	38.0%
Disagree a lot	132	21.0%	154	24.2%	76	15.4%	100	19.6%
Missing	2	.3%	4	.7%	2	.4%	1	.2%

Table 4.2   Interest or boredom in lessons: the responses of boys and girls compared

	Primary				Secondary			
	Boys		Girls		Boys		Girls	
Total	628	100%	635	100%	495	100%	508	100%
The work I do in lessons is interesting to me								
All lessons	111	17.6%	128	20.2%	60	12.2%	71	14.1%
Most lessons	297	47.3%	296	46.7%	255	51.6%	238	46.9%
Some lessons	183	29.2%	182	28.7%	154	31.1%	174	34.3%
Hardly any lessons	28	4.4%	18	2.9%	14	2.9%	17	3.4%
No lessons	6	.9%	6	.9%	10	2.0%	5	1.0%
Missing	4	.6%	4	.7%	1	.2%	2	.4%
I am bored in lessons								
All lessons	22	3.5%	10	1.6%	12	2.5%	9	1.7%
Most lessons	47	7.4%	20	3.2%	31	6.2%	31	6.1%
Some lessons	293	46.6%	234	36.9%	229	46.3%	233	45.9%
Hardly any lessons	193	30.8%	262	41.3%	184	37.2%	196	38.7%
No lessons	71	11.2%	104	16.4%	38	7.7%	39	7.6%
Missing	2	.4%	5	.7%	–	–	–	–
In a lesson, I often count the minutes till breaktime								
All lessons	138	21.9%	64	10.1%	57	11.5%	30	5.8%
Most lessons	99	15.7%	86	13.5%	62	12.6%	67	13.2%
Some lessons	165	26.3%	209	32.9%	177	35.7%	204	40.2%
Hardly any lessons	118	18.9%	164	25.8%	113	22.9%	136	26.9%
No lessons	105	16.8%	112	17.6%	85	17.2%	70	13.8%
Missing	3	.4%	0	.1%	1	.2%	1	.2%

Table 4.3 **The value of school and school work: the responses of boys and girls compared**

	Primary				Secondary			
	Boys		**Girls**		**Boys**		**Girls**	
Total	628	100%	635	100%	495	100%	508	100%
School work is worth doing								
Agree a lot	257	40.9%	311	49.0%	192	38.7%	195	38.4%
Agree	309	49.1%	280	44.1%	265	53.5%	276	54.3%
Not sure	33	5.2%	27	4.2%	12	2.4%	13	2.6%
Disagree	14	2.2%	5	.8%	14	2.8%	9	1.9%
Disagree a lot	11	1.7%	9	1.4%	10	2.1%	11	2.2%
Missing	5	.7%	3	.5%	2	.5%	3	.7%
The work I do in lessons is a waste of time								
All lessons	13	2.0%	8	1.3%	7	1.3%	2	.4%
Most lessons	18	2.8%	9	1.5%	7	1.4%	9	1.9%
Some lessons	79	12.7%	49	7.7%	57	11.6%	56	11.1%
Hardly any lessons	183	29.2%	141	22.2%	158	31.9%	166	32.7%
No lessons	328	52.3%	423	66.6%	261	52.7%	271	53.4%
Missing	7	1.1%	5	.8%	5	1.1%	3	.6%
School is a waste of time for me								
Agree a lot	9	1.4%	8	1.3%	8	1.7%	–	–
Agree	12	1.8%	8	1.3%	11	2.2%	12	2.5%
Not sure	38	6.1%	21	3.3%	20	4.1%	20	4.0%
Disagree	174	27.8%	126	19.8%	148	30.0%	157	31.0%
Disagree a lot	393	62.5%	470	74.1%	306	61.8%	316	62.3%
Missing	2	.4%	2	.3%	1	.2%	1	.2%

Table 4.4 Pupils' perceptions of the purposes of school: the responses of boys and girls compared

	Primary				Secondary			
	Boys		Girls		Boys		Girls	
Total	628	100%	635	100%	495	100%	508	100%
Schools should help us to do as well as possible in tests and in exams (like GCSE)								
Agree a lot	399	63.6%	447	70.4%	366	73.9%	408	80.4%
Agree	189	30.1%	168	26.5%	116	23.5%	85	16.8%
Not sure	21	3.4%	10	1.6%	7	1.4%	8	1.6%
Disagree	11	1.7%	6	1.0%	3	.6%	4	.8%
Disagree a lot	7	1.1%	3	.5%	1	.2%	1	.2%
Missing	2	.3%	–	–	2	.4%	2	.3%
Schools should teach things that will be useful when we get jobs								
Agree a lot	435	69.3%	418	65.9%	342	69.1%	381	75.0%
Agree	153	24.4%	168	26.5%	135	27.3%	112	22.1%
Not sure	18	2.9%	34	5.3%	9	1.8%	13	2.5%
Disagree	14	2.2%	10	1.6%	7	1.5%	2	.4%
Disagree a lot	2	.3%	1	.1%	1	.2%	–	–
Missing	6	.9%	3	.5%	–	–	–	–
Schools should help me to be independent and stand on my own two feet								
Agree a lot	283	45.1%	292	46.0%	200	40.3%	223	44.0%
Agree	256	40.8%	255	40.2%	237	48.0%	244	48.1%
Not sure	52	8.3%	48	7.6%	36	7.3%	25	5.0%,
Disagree	18	2.9%	26	4.1%	18	3.6%	13	2.5%
Disagree a lot	11	1.7%	8	1.3%	4	.8%	1	.2%
Missing	7	1.2%	4	.7%	–	–	1	.2%
Schools should help us to learn how to use our spare/leisure time								
Agree a lot	152	24.3%	114	17.9%	86	17.5%	65	12.7%,
Agree	202	32.2%	239	37.6%	189	38.1%	171	33.6%
Not sure	103	16.4%	136	21.4%	50	10.2%	78	15.4%
Disagree	105	16.7%	99	15.6%	108	21.9%	136	26.7%
Disagree a lot	61	9.8%	46	7.3%	60	12.1%	57	11.3%
Missing	4	.6%	2	.3%	1	.2%	1	.2%
School work doesn't help you get a job								
Agree a lot	19	3.0%	12	1.9%	9	1.9%	9	1.8%
Agree	18	2.9%	23	3.6%	15	3.1%	10	2.0%
Not sure	35	5.5%	37	5.9%	23	4.6%	16	3.1%
Disagree	143	22.7%	133	21.0%	123	24.9%	141	27.8%
Disagree a lot	408	65.0%	427	67.3%	324	65.5%	330	65.0%
Missing	5	.8%	2	.3%	–	–	2	.3%

Table 4.5   Perceived reputation of their school: the responses of boys and girls compared

	Primary				Secondary			
	Boys		Girls		Boys		Girls	
Total	628	100%	635	100%	495	100%	508	100%
People think this is a good school								
Agree a lot	245	39.1%	288	45.4%	185	37.4%	197	38.8%
Agree	263	41.8%	249	39.2%	249	50.4%	232	45.6%
Not sure	75	11.9%	73	11.5%	35	7.2%	59	11.7%
Disagree	25	4.0%	12	1.8%	20	4.0%	12	2.3%
Disagree a lot	15	2.3%	7	1.0%	5	1.1%	6	1.2%
Missing	5	.8%	7	1.1%	–	–	2	.3%
My school is clean and tidy								
Always......................................	214	34.1%	288	45.4%	74	15.0%	119	23.5%
Nearly always	275	43.8%	276	43.5%	243	49.2%	256	50.3%
Sometimes	114	18.2%	59	9.4%	113	22.9%	107	21.1%
Hardly ever...............................	11	1.7%	4	.6%	27	5.4%	18	3.5%
Never	13	2.1%	7	1.0%	32	6.5%	8	1.6%
Missing	1	.2%	1	.2%	5	1.0%	–	–

Table 4.6   Liking for teachers: the responses of boys and girls compared

	Primary				Secondary			
	Boys		Girls		Boys		Girls	
Total	628	100%	635	100%	495	100%	508	100%
I like my teacher(s)								
Always......................................	231	36.8%	308	48.5%	65	13.1%	91	17.9%
Nearly always	182	29.0%	191	30.1%	198	40.0%	183	36.1%
Sometimes	153	24.4%	101	16.0%	192	38.7%	201	39.7%
Hardly ever...............................	31	5.0%	13	2.1%	20	4.0%	25	4.9%
Never	27	4.4%	19	2.9%	21	4.2%	7	1.4%
Missing	3	.4%	3	.4%	–	–	–	–

Table 4.7 Ensuring the quality of pupils' work: the responses of boys and girls compared

	Primary				Secondary			
	Boys		Girls		Boys		Girls	
Total	628	100%	635	100%	495	100%	508	100%
My teacher(s):								
always marks my work	342	54.5%	376	59.3%	195	39.4%	166	32.7%
usually marks my work	262	41.8%	250	39.3%	279	56.4%	313	61.6%
hardly ever marks my work	22	3.5%	7	1.0%	20	4.1%	27	5.4%
Missing	2	.3%	2	.3%	1	.2%	1	.2%
My teacher(s) makes sure we do any homework that is set								
Always	383	61.0%	403	63.5%	271	54.7%	300	59.1%
Nearly always	150	24.0%	140	22.1%	182	36.8%	174	34.3%
Sometimes	63	10.0%	61	9.6%	30	6.1%	27	5.4%
Hardly ever	12	1.9%	13	2.0%	7	1.3%	6	1.2%
Never	12	2.0%	10	1.5%	6	1.1%	–	–
Missing	7	1.1%	8	1.3%	–	–	–	–
My teacher(s):								
tries hard to make me work as well								
as I am able	536	85.4%	544	85.7%	387	78.2%	388	76.4%
is fairly easily satisfied	81	13.0%	85	13.4%	95	19.2%	110	21.7%
doesn't seem to care whether								
I work or not	9	1.4%	4	.6%	9	1.8%	9	1.9%
Missing	2	.3%	2	.3%	4	.8%	–	–
My teacher(s) tells me when I do my school work well								
Always	310	49.4%	311	48.9%	230	46.5%	222	43.7%
Nearly always	202	32.2%	207	32.6%	189	38.2%	193	38.1%
Sometimes	91	14.4%	104	16.3%	54	11.0%	70	13.8%
Hardly ever	15	2.3%	5	.8%	15	3.0%	17	3.4%
Never	9	1.5%	6	.9%	4	.8%	5	1.0%
Missing	1	.2%	3	.4%	2	.4%	–	–

Table 4.8 Maintaining discipline: the responses of boys and girls compared

	Primary				Secondary			
	Boys		**Girls**		**Boys**		**Girls**	
Total	628	100%	635	100%	495	100%	508	100%
The teachers in my school take action *when they see anyone breaking school rules*								
Always..................................	406	64.7%	401	63.1%	304	61.3%	333	65.7%
Nearly always	163	26.0%	176	27.7%	151	30.4%	142	28.0%
Sometimes	39	6.2%	44	6.9%	29	5.8%	30	5.9%
Hardly ever..............................	12	1.9%	9	1.5%	8	1.6%	2	.4%
Never	5	.8%	3	.4%	3	.6%	–	–
Missing	2	.4%	2	.4%	1	.2%	–	–
My teacher(s) makes it clear how we *should behave in school*								
Always..................................	472	75.2%	509	80.2%	363	73.3%	373	73.5%
Nearly always	110	17.6%	91	14.4%	103	20.8%	109	21.4%
Sometimes	32	5.1%	25	4.0%	26	5.3%	23	4.6%
Hardly ever..............................	3	.5%	6	1.0%	2	.4%	1	.2%
Never	7	1.2%	1	.2%	1	.2%	–	–
Missing	3	.5%	1	.2%	–	–	1	.2%
My teacher(s) can control the class								
Always..................................	311	49.5%	382	60.1%	114	23.1%	124	24.4%
Nearly always	198	31.5%	173	27.3%	246	49.7%	212	41.7%
Sometimes	83	13.2%	57	8.9%	102	20.6%	135	26.6%
Hardly ever..............................	20	3.3%	8	1.2%	19	3.9%	22	4.4%
Never	15	2.4%	13	2.0%	11	2.2%	14	2.8%
Missing	1	.2%	3	.4%	3	.6%	1	.2%
My school has sensible rules								
Agree a lot	229	36.5%	254	40.0%	147	29.7%	124	24.4%
Agree	306	48.7%	305	48.0%	283	57.1%	294	57.9%
Not sure	43	6.9%	41	6.4%	22	4.5%	40	8.0%
Disagree	41	6.6%	32	5.1%	33	6.6%	43	8.6%
Disagree a lot	8	1.2%	3	.4%	10	2.0%	5	1.0%
Missing	1	.1%	–	–	–	–	1	.2%
Do you think the discipline in your school is:								
too strict?	39	6.3%	24	3.8%	71	14.4%	58	11.4%
about right?	556	88.5%	586	92.3%	406	82.0%	421	82.9%
not strict enough?	28	4.4%	20	3.2%	17	3.4%	28	5.4%
Missing	5	.9%	4	.6%	1	.2%	2	.3%
Does your school have:								
too many rules?	123	19.6%	68	10.7%	146	29.5%	111	21.8%
about the right number of rules? ..	472	75.2%	527	83.1%	330	66.7%	380	74.9%
not enough rules?	28	4.5%	37	5.9%	16	3.2%	16	3.2%
Missing	5	.8%	2	.4%	3	.6%	1	.1%

Table 4.9 Talking individually to teachers: the responses of boys and girls compared

	Primary				Secondary			
	Boys		**Girls**		**Boys**		**Girls**	
Total	628	100%	635	100%	495	100%	508	100%
Have you talked to your class teacher about your work this year?								
Yes, often	49	7.8%	59	9.3%	46	9.3%	33	6.6%
Yes, sometimes	252	40.1%	223	35.2%	203	41.0%	214	42.1%
No, never	325	51.8%	350	55.2%	237	47.8%	247	48.7%
Missing	2	.3%	2	.3%	10	1.9%	13	2.6%
Have you talked to other teachers about your work?								
Yes, often	NA	NA	NA	NA	45	9.2%	34	6.7%
Yes, sometimes	NA	NA	NA	NA	202	40.9%	201	39.6%
No, never	NA	NA	NA	NA	237	47.9%	263	51.9%
Missing	NA	NA	NA	NA	11	2.0%	10	1.9%

Table 4.10 Types of lessons liked: the responses of boys and girls compared

	Primary				Secondary			
	Boys		Girls		Boys		Girls	
Total	628	100%	635	100%	495	100%	508	100%
I like lessons where I can work with my friends								
Agree a lot	435	69.2%	397	62.5%	306	61.9%	318	62.7%
Agree	157	24.9%	177	27.9%	171	34.6%	162	31.9%
Not sure	6	.9%	36	5.6%	6	1.2%	12	2.4%
Disagree	12	1.9%	13	2.1%	7	1.5%	13	2.6%
Disagree a lot	15	2.4%	12	1.9%	3	.6%	2	.3%
Missing	4	.6%	–	–	1	.2%	1	.1%
I like lessons where I can work on my own								
Agree a lot	99	15.7%	135	21.3%	55	11.0%	84	16.5%
Agree	206	32.8%	218	34.4%	205	41.5%	201	39.6%
Not sure	100	15.9%	99	15.6%	57	11.4%	47	9.2%
Disagree	134	21.3%	111	17.5%	108	21.9%	118	23.3%
Disagree a lot	86	13.7%	68	10.7%	69	14.0%	56	11.0%
Missing	4	.6%	3	.5%	1	.2%	2	.4%
I like lessons where I can make something								
Agree a lot	433	69.0%	369	58.2%	307	62.0%	251	49.5%
Agree	156	24.8%	207	32.5%	155	31.3%	206	40.5%
Not sure	21	3.3%	30	4.7%	12	2.4%	18	3.5%
Disagree	10	1.6%	14	2.3%	17	3.3%	24	4.7%
Disagree a lot	6	.9%	12	1.9%	5	1.0%	9	1.7%
Missing	3	.5%	2	.4%	–	–	–	–
I like lessons where we talk about our ideas								
Agree a lot	235	37.4%	211	33.3%	160	32.3%	153	30.2%
Agree	251	40.0%	273	43.1%	236	47.7%	252	49.6%
Not sure	50	8.0%	58	9.1%	31	6.2%	40	7.9%
Disagree	57	9.1%	68	10.7%	52	10.5%	39	7.8%
Disagree a lot	32	5.1%	23	3.6%	17	3.4%	22	4.4%
Missing	2	.4%	2	.3%	–	–	1	.1%

Table 4.11 Perceptions of ability and perserverence: the responses of boys and girls compared

	Primary				Secondary			
	Boys		**Girls**		**Boys**		**Girls**	
Total	628	100%	635	100%	495	100%	508	100%
I work as hard as I can in school								
All lessons	179	28.6%	240	37.9%	112	22.6%	191	37.6%
Most lessons	315	50.1%	334	52.7%	303	61.3%	259	50.9%
Some lessons	118	18.8%	59	9.2%	69	13.9%	54	10.6%
Hardly any lessons	8	1.3%	0	.1%	7	1.4%	2	.4%
No lessons	3	.5%	1	.1%	3	.7%	1	.2%
Missing	4	.6%	–	–	1	.2%	2	.3%
How good do you think you are at school work?								
Better than most of my class	106	16.9%	83	13.0%	80	16.2%	62	12.2%
As good as most of my class	378	60.1%	454	71.5%	358	72.4%	384	75.7%
Not as good as most of my class ..	136	21.7%	95	15.0%	54	10.9%	57	11.3%
Missing	8	1.2%	3	.4%	2	.4%	4	.8%
I get good marks for my work								
All lessons	45	7.1%	42	6.6%	38	7.7%	42	8.4%
Most lessons	271	43.2%	303	47.8%	270	54.5%	285	56.1%
Some lessons	247	39.3%	252	39.7%	172	34.7%	163	32.0%
Hardly any lessons	51	8.1%	31	4.8%	9	1.8%	13	2.5%
No lessons	11	1.7%	6	.9%	4	.9%	4	.9%
Missing	4	.6%	1	.2%	2	.4%	1	.1%
How do you think your teachers would describe your school work?								
Better than most of my class	79	12.6%	75	11.8%	63	12.8%	59	11.7%
As good as most of my class	457	72.8%	490	77.2%	378	76.3%	389	76.6%
Not as good as most of my class ..	86	13.7%	63	9.9%	49	10.0%	53	10.5%
Missing	5	.8%	7	1.1%	5	1.0%	6	1.2%

Table 4.12 Behaviour in school this year: the responses of boys and girls compared

	Primary				Secondary			
	Boys		Girls		Boys		Girls	
Total	628	100%	635	100%	495	100%	508	100%
Describe your behaviour in class and around school this year								
Always well behaved	57	9.0%	123	19.4%	52	10.5%	99	19.5%
Usually well behaved	383	61.0%	423	66.6%	317	64.1%	340	66.9%
Sometimes badly behaved	164	26.2%	76	12.0%	114	23.0%	63	12.3%
Often badly behaved	20	3.1%	11	1.7%	7	1.5%	6	1.2%
Missing	4	.6%	2	.3%	5	1.0%	1	.1%
How often have you had punishments this year?								
Never	189	30.1%	377	59.4%	144	29.2%	274	53.9%
Once or twice	347	55.2%	226	35.6%	285	57.5%	202	39.7%
Quite often	63	10.1%	18	2.8%	39	7.8%	22	4.3%
Often	27	4.2%	8	1.3%	24	4.8%	9	1.8%
Missing	2	.4%	6	.9%	3	.6%	1	.2%

Table 4.13 Truancy: the responses of boys and girls compared

	Primary				Secondary			
	Boys		Girls		Boys		Girls	
Total	628	100%	635	100%	495	100%	508	100%
How often have you played truant this year?								
One or two lessons, occasionally .	15	2.5%	4	.7%	23	4.6%	11	2.1%
A whole day, occasionally	31	5.0%	24	3.8%	27	5.5%	15	2.9%
Several days at a time	2	.4%	3	.4%	7	1.3%	–	–
Weeks at a time	5	.8%	5	.7%	2	.4%	3	.6%
I have not played truant	570	90.7%	596	93.9%	435	87.8%	476	93.8%
Missing	4	.7%	3	.5%	2	.4%	3	.5%

Table 4.14 Bullying: the responses of boys and girls compared

	Primary				Secondary			
	Boys		**Girls**		**Boys**		**Girls**	
Total	628	100%	635	100%	495	100%	508	100%
Have you even been bullied in school this year?								
Never	317	50.4%	294	46.3%	209	42.3%	231	45.4%
Once or twice	219	34.9%	231	36.4%	227	45.9%	220	43.3%
Quite often	53	8.4%	72	11.3%	35	7.2%	41	8.1%
Often	37	5.9%	35	5.5%	20	4.1%	14	2.7%
Missing	3	.4%	4	.6%	2	.5%	2	.4%

Table 4.15 School-related activities: the responses of boys and girls compared

	Primary				Secondary			
	Boys		**Girls**		**Boys**		**Girls**	
Total	628	100%	635	100%	495	100%	508	100%
Do you take part in any lunch hour or after school activities?								
Yes	477	76.0%	450	70.8%	329	66.4%	298	58.7%
No	98	15.5%	122	19.2%	136	27.5%	184	36.3%
There are no lunch hour or after school activities	51	8.1%	61	9.6%	25	5.0%	18	3.5%
Missing	2	.3%	2	.4%	5	1.1%	7	1.5%
How many hours per day do you normally spend doing homework?								
I am not usually given homework...	274	43.7%	264	41.6%	18	3.6%	9	1.7%
I am given homework but I don't do it	26	4.2%	15	2.4%	14	2.9%	8	1.7%
Half hour or less	152	24.3%	152	23.9%	122	24.6%	79	15.6%
About 1 hour	107	17.1%	98	15.5%	196	39.5%	197	38.8%
About 1 and a half hours	26	4.1%	49	7.7%	81	16.3%	115	22.6%
About 2 hours	18	2.8%	18	2.9%	40	8.1%	50	9.9%
About 2 and a half hours	7	1.1%	10	1.5%	7	1.5%	15	3.0%
3 hours or more	2	.3%	11	1.7%	6	1.3%	13	2.6%
Missing	16	2.5%	18	2.8%	11	2.2%	20	4.0%
Homework is important in helping me to do well at school								
Agree a lot	301	47.9%	287	45.3%	194	39.1%	217	42.7%
Agree	227	36.2%	265	41.8%	223	45.0%	222	43.7%
Not sure	56	8.9%	58	9.2%	19	3.8%	25	5.0%
Disagree	29	4.7%	19	3.0%	44	8.8%	37	7.3%
Disagree a lot	15	2.4%	4	.6%	16	3.3%	7	1.4%
Missing	–	–	1	.2%	–	–	–	–

Table 4.16 Leisure activities: the responses of boys and girls compared

	Primary				Secondary			
	Boys		**Girls**		**Boys**		**Girls**	
Total	628	100%	635	100%	495	100%	508	100%
How often do you read on your own for fun outside school?								
(Almost) every day	215	34.2%	361	56.9%	140	28.2%	240	47.3%
Once or twice a week	193	30.8%	164	25.8%	159	32.2%	156	30.7%
Once or twice a month	96	15.3%	38	6.1%	101	20.4%	53	10.4%
Never or hardly ever	116	18.5%	68	10.7%	90	18.1%	54	10.6%
Missing	8	1.2%	4	.6%	5	1.0%	5	.9%
How many hours each day do you watch television/videos?								
I don't watch television/videos	15	2.5%	12	1.8%	9	1.9%	8	1.5%
Up to 1 hour	117	18.7%	133	20.9%	83	16.8%	82	16.2%
About 2 hours	165	26.2%	167	26.3%	120	24.2%	133	26.2%
About 3 hours	131	20.8%	147	23.2%	101	20.4%	118	23.2%
About 4 hours	68	10.9%	75	11.9%	86	17.4%	75	14.8%
About 5 hours	41	6.5%	37	5.8%	37	7.4%,	44	8.6%
6 hours or more	88	14.1%	52	8.1%	52	10.6%	42	8.2%
Missing	3	.4%	12	1.9%	7	1.4%	7	1.4%
How many hours each day do you play computer games?								
I don't play computer games	72	11.5%	197	31.0%	69	14.0%	185	36.4%
Up to 1 hour	252	40.1%	289	45.6%	207	41.8%	226	44.5%
About 2 hours	116	18.4%	83	13.1%	89	17.9%	57	11.3%
About 3 hours	68	10.8%	21	3.3%	54	11.0%	21	4.1%
About 4 hours	38	6.0%	12	1.9%	23	4.7%	2	.5%
About 5 hours	16	2.5%	8	1.2%	10	2.0%	1	.2%
6 hours or more	53	8.4%	8	1.2%	33	6.7%	9	1.8%
Missing	15	2.3%	17	2.6%	9	1.8%	6	1.2%

Table 4.17 Parents' opinions about the value of education: the responses of boys and girls compared

	Primary				Secondary			
	Boys		**Girls**		**Boys**		**Girls**	
Total	628	100%	635	100%	495	100%	508	100%
My parents think it is important for me to do well at school								
Agree a lot	532	84.7%	529	83.4%	424	85.7%	422	83.0%
Agree	86	13.6%	90	14.2%	62	12.5%	80	15.8%
Not sure	3	.4%	8	1.2%	4	.8%	4	.7%
Disagree	3	.5%	5	.8%	2	.4%	–	–
Disagree a lot	3	.5%	1	.2%	2	.4%	–	–
Missing	1	.2%	1	.1%	1	.2%	2	.4%
My parents think school is a waste of time								
Agree a lot	3	.5%	6	1.0%	4	.8%	3	.6%
Agree	5	.8%	1	.2%	4	.8%	1	.2%
Not sure	26	4.2%	14	2.1%	7	1.5%	11	2.1%
Disagree	74	11.8%	49	7.7%	53	10.7%	52	10.3%
Disagree a lot	519	82.7%	563	88.7%	427	86.2%	441	86.9%
Missing	–	–	1	.2%	–	–	–	–

Table 4.18 Parental interest and support: the responses of boys and girls compared

	Primary				Secondary			
	Boys		**Girls**		**Boys**		**Girls**	
Total	628	100%	635	100%	495	100%	508	100%
What do you think that your parents want you to do?								
Go into the sixth form of this school ..	NA	NA	NA	NA	177	35.8%	198	39.1%
Go to another school or college ...	NA	NA	NA	NA	132	26.6%	166	32.7%
Get a job as soon as possible	NA	NA	NA	NA	54	10.9%	20	4.0%
Not sure	NA	NA	NA	NA	123	24.9%	109	21.5%
Missing	NA	NA	NA	NA	9	1.8%	14	2.7%
My parents are interested in how I do at school								
Always	471	75.1%	498	78.4%	393	79.3%	399	78.6%
Nearly always	105	16.8%	90	14.1%	67	13.6%	77	15.1%
Sometimes	39	6.3%	37	5.8%	28	5.7%	27	5.3%
Hardly ever..............................	5	.8%	7	1.1%	3	.6%	3	.6%
Never	6	.9%	3	.5%	1	.2%	–	–
Missing	1	.2%	0	.1%	2	.4%	2	.4%
My parents come to school parents' evenings								
Always	413	65.8%	443	69.7%	297	60.0%	332	65.3%
Nearly always	139	22.2%	129	20.3%	130	26.3%	106	20.9%
Sometimes	52	8.2%	47	7.4%	44	8.9%	45	8.9%
Hardly ever..............................	9	1.5%	12	1.9%	11	2.3%	11	2.2%
Never	11	1.8%	4	.6%	12	2.3%	11	2.1%
Missing	4	.6%	–	–	1	.2%	3	.6%
My parents make it clear that I should behave myself in school								
Agree a lot	340	54.1%	360	56.6%	267	53.9%	263	51.8%
Agree	239	38.1%	239	37.6%	197	39.8%	214	42.1%
Not sure	29	4.6%	19	3.0%	17	3.5%	15	2.9%
Disagree	14	2.3%	13	2.1%	13	2.6%	13	2.5%
Disagree a lot	1	.2%	2	.3%	1	.2%	2	.4%
Missing	5	.8%	2	.3%	–	–	1	.2%
My parents make sure I do my homework								
Always	423	67.3%	453	71.3%	331	66.9%	347	68.3%
Nearly always	115	18.3%	111	17.5%	97	19.6%	99	19.4%
Sometimes	52	8.3%	43	6.8%	42	8.4%	51	10.0%
Hardly ever..............................	12	1.9%	9	1.4%	13	2.5%	6	1.1%
Never	20	3.2%	12	1.8%	12	2.4%	4	.8%
Missing	6	.9%	7	1.2%	1	.2%	2	.4%

Table 4.19 Post-16 intentions: the responses of boys and girls compared

	Primary				Secondary			
	Boys		Girls		Boys		Girls	
Total	628	100%	635	100%	495	100%	508	100%
After taking exams at the end of Year 11 do you expect to:								
go into the sixth form of this school/your secondary school?	160	25.5%	176	27.7%	143	29.0%	160	31.5%
go to another school or college? ..	142	22.6%	171	27.0%	125	25.4%	167	32.8%
get a job as soon as possible?	118	18.8%	60	9.4%	87	17.6%	32	6.3%
Not sure	207	33.0%	221	34.7%	134	27.0%	141	27.8%
Missing	1	.1%	7	1.1%	5	1.1%	8	1.5%

CHAPTER 5

PUPILS WHO DON'T LIKE SCHOOL

5.1   Introduction

The purpose of the chapter is to compare the responses of the minority of pupils who said they disliked school with those of the majority of pupils who liked school. A small number of key questions in the pupil questionnaire have been selected for these comparisons. These key questions were selected on the basis of the results of multilevel analyses described in our earlier study into pupils' attitudes towards school (Keys and Fernandes, 1993) and of the previous research reviewed by Keys and Fernandes (op. cit.).

Each pupil's response to the statement 'On the whole I like being at school' was selected as the best measure of whether or not s/he liked school. Pupils who 'agreed a lot' or 'agreed' with this statement were deemed to *like* school and those who 'disagreed' or 'disagreed a lot' were deemed to *dislike* school; the small number of pupils who had selected the 'not sure' option for this statement were excluded from the comparisons.

Using these criteria, in the primary school sample the group who *liked* school consisted of 1022 pupils and the group who *disliked* school consisted of 94 pupils. In the secondary school sample, the totals were 829 pupils and 97 pupils respectively. The groups who were 'not sure' consisted of 140 primary and 80 secondary school pupils; as noted above, these pupils were excluded from the analyses. It is important to note that the groups who *disliked* school in both samples represented *fewer than one in ten of all the pupils* (eight per cent of the primary school pupils and ten per cent of the secondary sample).

At each age group the pupils who *disliked* school were compared with those who *liked* school in terms of their responses to the following statements or questions:

   'I am bored in lessons'

   'School is a waste of time for me'

   'The work I do in school is a waste of time'

   'I like my teachers'

   'I work as hard as I can in school'

'I get good marks for my work'

'How would you describe your behaviour in class and around school this year?'

'Homework is important in helping me to do well at school'

'My parents are interested in how I do at school'

'My parents make sure I do my homework'.

5.2 Boredom

Previous research suggests that there is a relationship between dislike of school and boredom with school work (Keys and Fernandes, 1993). This relationship is well illustrated in Figure 5.1, which shows that the pupils who *disliked* school were far more likely than those who *liked* school to say they were bored in lessons. Over a third of the pupils who *disliked* school said they were bored in 'all' or 'most lessons' compared with only five per cent of those who *liked* school. On the other hand, over half of the pupils who *liked* school said that they were 'never' or 'hardly ever bored' in lessons compared with 10 - 14 per cent of the pupils who *disliked* school. The patterns of response were similar for top primary and first-year secondary pupils.

Figure 5.1   *'I am bored in lessons'* : the responses compared of pupils who *like* and *dislike* school

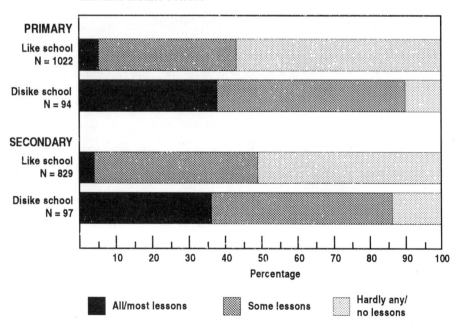

81

5.3 The value of school and school work

The analyses carried out in our previous study (Keys and Fernandes, op. cit.) identified a strong association between disliking school and placing a low value on school and school work. This is illustrated in Figures 5.2 and 5.3.

Figure 5.2 *'The work I do in lessons is a waste of time'* : the responses compared of pupils who *like* and *dislike* school

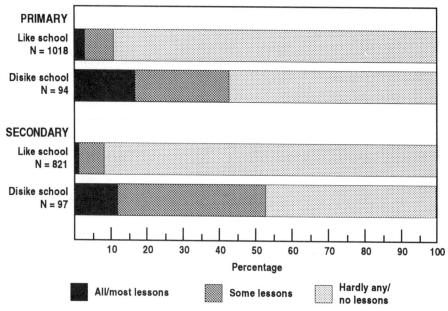

Figure 5.3 *'School is a waste of time for me'* : the responses compared of pupils who *like* and *dislike* school

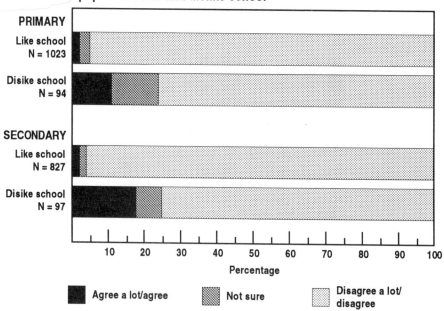

About ninety per cent of the pupils who *liked* school indicated that in 'hardly any' or 'no lessons' was 'the work I do in lessons . . . a waste of time'. The responses of the pupils who *disliked* school, on the other hand, are quite different: only about half expressed this view and a fairly substantial minority (17 per cent of top primary and 12 per cent of first-year secondary) indicated that the work they did in 'all' or 'most lessons' was a waste of time (Figure 5.2).

A similar picture is revealed by Figure 5.3: whereas almost all (95 and 96 per cent) of the pupils who *liked* school disagreed with the statement that 'School is a waste of time for me', only about three-quarters of those who *disliked* school expressed this view.

5.4 Like and dislike for teachers

Our earlier study (Keys and Fernandes, op. cit.) and the previous research reviewed there demonstrated a link between liking for teachers and liking for school. This is illustrated by Figure 5.4, which shows that, amongst primary and secondary school pupils, those who *disliked* school were far less likely to like their teachers than those who said they *liked* school. Nearly 80 per cent of the primary school children who *liked* school also liked their teacher, compared with fewer than 40 per cent of those who *disliked* school. Comparable figures for the secondary school pupils reveal a similar difference: 60 per cent of those who *liked* school also liked their teachers, compared with fewer than 20 per cent of those who *disliked* school.

Figure 5.4   *'I like my teacher(s)'* : the responses compared of pupils who like and *dislike* school

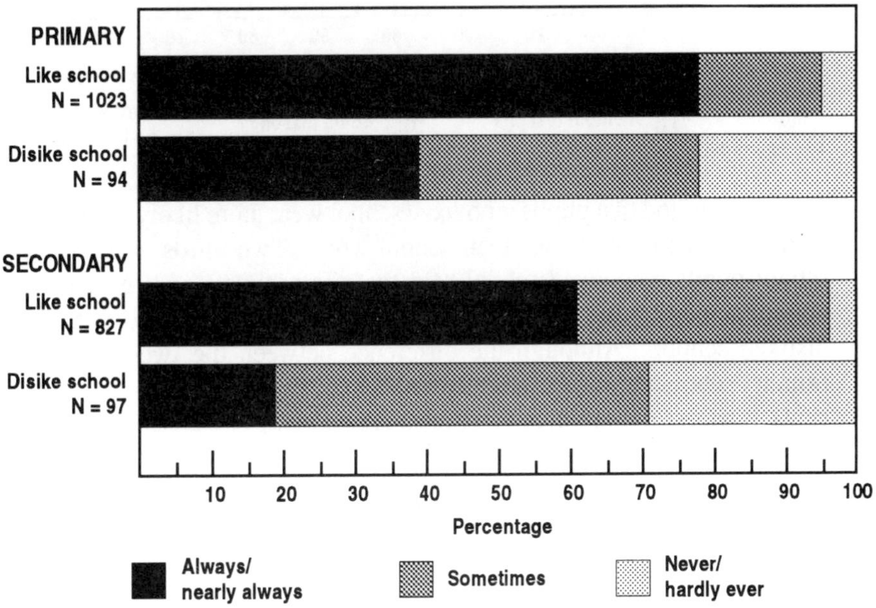

5.5 Working hard and getting good marks

Our previous research (Keys and Fernandes, op. cit.) demonstrated that pupils who *liked* school tended to perceive themselves as hard working and high achieving. In addition, the previous research we reviewed confirmed the link between achievement and positive attitudes towards school. These relationships are illustrated in Figures 5.5 and 5.6.

Figure 5.5 shows that pupils who say they like school are also more likely to say that they work hard in 'all' or 'most lessons'. About 90 per cent of the primary and secondary school pupils who *liked* school said that they worked hard in all/most lessons compared with about 60 per cent of those who *disliked* school.

Figure 5.5   *'I work as hard as I can in school'* : the responses compared of pupils who *like* and *dislike* school

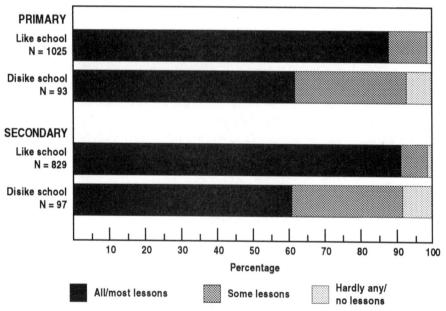

This study found that pupils who *liked* school were more likely to say that they were given good marks for their school work. Two-thirds of the secondary school pupils who *liked* school said that they 'always' or 'nearly always' obtained good marks for their work, compared with one-third of those who disliked school. Although the difference between the two groups within primary school pupils was slightly smaller (57 per cent compared with 35 per cent), it was still more than 20 percentage points.

Figure 5.6 *'I get good marks for my work'* : the responses compared of pupils who *like* and *dislike* school

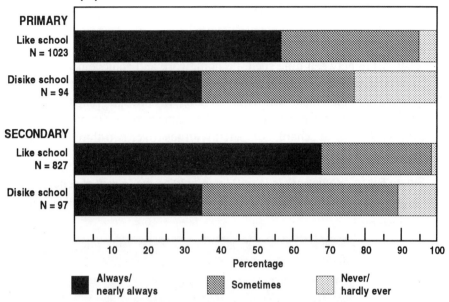

Always/ nearly always   Sometimes   Never/ hardly ever

5.6 Behaviour in school

Our previous study (Keys and Fernandes, op. cit.) found a link between good behaviour and positive attitudes towards school. This is illustrated in Figure 5.7, which shows that pupils who *like* school tend to perceive themselves as better behaved than those who *dislike* school. Over 85 per cent of the secondary school pupils who *liked* school said that they were 'always' or 'usually well-behaved' compared with just over half of those who *disliked* school; comparable figures for primary school pupils were 80 per cent and just over 60 per cent.

Figure 5.7 *'Describe your behaviour in class and around school this year'* : the responses compared of pupils who *like* and *dislike* school

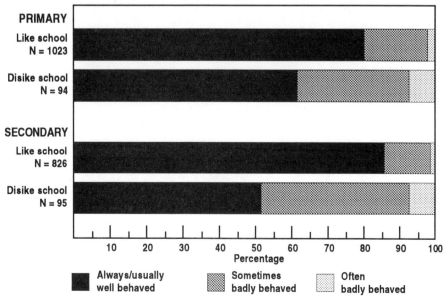

Always/usually well behaved   Sometimes badly behaved   Often badly behaved

5.7 Views on homework

The earlier study (Keys and Fernandes, op. cit.) found a positive correlation between time spent on homework and positive attitudes towards school. In addition, other studies (Lapointe *et al.*, 1992, for example) have identified a relationship between time spent on homework and achievement. Figure 5.8 shows that pupils who *like* school are more likely to believe in the importance of homework than those who *dislike* school. In both age groups, nearly 90 per cent of pupils who *liked* school agreed that homework was important in helping them to do well at school, compared with just over two-thirds of those who *disliked* school.

Figure 5.8   *'Homework is important in helping me to well at school'* : the responses compared of pupils who *like* and *dislike* school

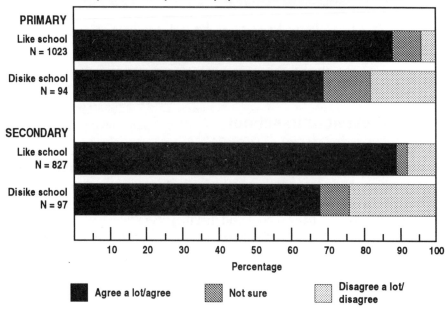

5.8 Parental support

Our previous research (Keys and Fernandes, op. cit.) demonstrated a link between pupils' perceptions of parental support and their attitudes towards school. These links are illustrated in Figures 5.9 and 5.10, which show the pupils' responses to statements concerned with parental support. The pattern of response is similar for both statements: in both age groups about 90 per cent of the pupils who *liked* school and about 80 per cent of those who *disliked* school agreed that their parents were 'always' or 'nearly always' interested in how they did at school and always/nearly always made sure they did their homework. However, the difference between the responses of pupils who *liked* and those who *disliked* school to these statements concerned with parental support (about 10 percentage points) was smaller than for the other statements illustrated in this chapter, most of which showed differences in excess of 20 percentage points. It may be that, although the majority of parents are interested and supportive, some parents are more adept than others at fostering positive attitudes towards school in their children. Halsey (1972), and Wedge and Prosser (1973), for example, found evidence of high parental interest and aspirations for their children in disadvantaged areas which did not appear to be translated into higher staying-on rates. It could also be that some schools may be more adept at helping parents to intervene more positively in their children's education.

Figure 5.9 *'My parents are interested in how I do at school'* : the responses compared of pupils who *like* and *dislike* school

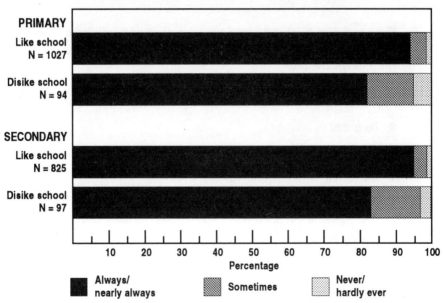

Figure 5.10 *'My parents make sure I do my homework'*: the responses compared of pupils who *like* and *dislike* school

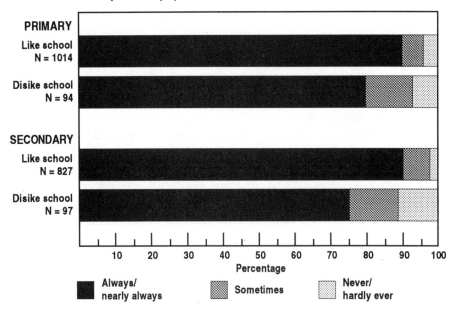

5.9 Summary

Figures 5.1 to 5.10 compared the responses of pupils who *disliked* school with those who *liked* school. The main conclusions are summarised below.

Pupils who *dislike* school were *more likely* to:

♦ be bored in lessons

♦ think that the work they did in lessons was a waste of time

♦ think that school was a waste of time

♦ dislike their teachers;

less likely to say that they:

♦ worked hard at school

♦ obtained good marks for their work

- behaved well in school

- believed homework was important;

and *slightly less likely* to:

- believe their parents were interested in how they did at school

- say that their parents made sure they did their homework.

However, although pupils who *liked* school were far more likely to express positive responses to the other statements, it should be borne in mind that some pupils who *disliked* school also responded positively. For example, about half of these pupils did not agree that school was a waste of time, over half said that they worked as hard as they could at school, nearly 40 per cent of those in the primary school said that they liked their teacher and over 80 per cent said that their parents were interested in how they did at school.

CHAPTER 6
OVERVIEW AND IMPLICATIONS

6.1   Introduction

The research described in the preceding chapters compared the attitudes towards school and learning of about 2250 top primary and first-year secondary school pupils in 79 randomly selected schools (38 primary and 41 secondary) in England and Wales. The survey took place during the summer term 1994. Data on pupils' attitudes were collected by means of a self-completion questionnaire administered to the pupils in their classrooms, usually by their own class or form teachers. Although most of the questions in the questionnaire were pre-coded, a small number of questions invited pupils to comment in their own words. In order to preserve confidentiality, each pupil was given an envelope in which to seal his/her questionnaire.

The main purposes of the study were:

♦   to throw more light on the ways in which pupils' attitudes towards school and learning evolve as they become older

♦   to test the hypothesis that pupils' attitudes deteriorate sharply after the transition from primary to secondary school

♦   to compare the attitudes towards school of girls and boys

♦   to highlight any common characteristics amongst the small group of pupils who said they disliked school.

The main topics covered in the questionnaire for pupils were their:

♦   attitudes towards school and learning

♦   perceptions of teachers and teaching

♦   self-reported behaviour in and out of school

♦   perceptions of parental interest and support.

6.2 Main findings

The findings of the research are summarised in detail at the end of each of the foregoing chapters. The main highlights are given below.

♦ *The majority of top primary and first-year secondary school pupils liked school and school work.*

♦ *The primary school pupils tended to hold slightly more positive attitudes than the first-year secondary pupils, but the study found no evidence of a dramatic deterioration of pupils' attitudes after transition to secondary school.*

♦ *In both year groups a minority of pupils – about ten per cent – expressed negative attitudes towards school and school work.*

♦ *Pupils who disliked school tended to be more likely to: find school work boring and consider it a waste of time; dislike their teachers; behave badly in class. They also tended to be less likely to have a positive academic self-image and perceived their parents as less supportive.*

♦ *Girls tended to hold slightly more positive attitudes than boys.*

6.3 Implications for schools

The fact that most pupils perceive their experiences at school, and with teachers, in a favourable light, despite the large number of developments and changes which have increased the pressure on teachers and pupils in recent years, will be reassuring for all those concerned with education.

Secondary schools will take heart from our finding that the results of our study do not support the popularly held view that pupils' attitudes towards school deteriorate sharply after transition to secondary school: the secondary school pupils taking part in this study had been in their new schools for almost one full academic year at the time of the survey (summer 1994).

Although we found that the attitudes of the first-year secondary school pupils were slightly less positive than those of the top primary pupils, the differences were not large. It should also be remembered that there are two significant factors that may affect the responses of the secondary school pupils. Firstly, being a year older, and thus slightly more mature in their outlook, they may be less inclined to express extreme views (i.e. select the most or least favourable options from a scale), but prefer to select a more cautious standpoint. Secondly, the transfer from primary to secondary school introduces pupils to a different type of school organisation, where they encounter perhaps more than ten different teachers during the course of a week for different subjects, as compared with the usual pattern of one class teacher in the primary school. Clearly, when responding to statements and questions about their teachers, most primary pupils would have one teacher in mind, whereas the secondary pupils would have had several teachers in mind. Their actual response thus represents a synthesis of their views concerning different teachers.

However, despite the fact that the majority of pupils clearly have positive views concerning school, we must acknowledge that there is a small proportion of pupils whose responses suggested that they were disaffected. Approximately one in ten pupils indicated that, on the whole, they disliked being at school: this was true even for the top primary pupils, who, as we have already seen, were frequently more positive in their responses than the older first-year secondary pupils. In practice, this means that in a typical class of 25-35 pupils, two or three could be expected to have negative attitudes towards school.

The results of our research may help schools to consider the needs of this small group of children. In terms of making school a positive experience for as many pupils as possible, the views expressed by the pupils surveyed in this study can be used to suggest some strategies that schools may wish to consider; some of these are described below.

6.3.1 In the classroom

Our study found that pupils who disliked school were more likely than those who liked school to say that school work was boring and that school was a waste of time. They were also less likely to say that they worked hard and obtained good marks for their work. Other studies (for example, Robinson, 1990; and Kinder *et al.,* 1995) have also demonstrated links between boredom with school, disaffection and poor achievement.

In their conclusions, Kinder *et al.* (op. cit.) highlight the importance of offering alternative curricular experiences to disaffected, and potentially disaffected, pupils. Our findings on the types of lessons pupils liked best may be useful in this regard. More than nine out of ten pupils from each age group indicated that they liked lessons where they could work with their friends. A similar proportion reported liking lessons where they could make something. Also popular were lessons where pupils had opportunities to talk about their ideas (liked by roughly 80 per cent of both samples). Conversely, about one in three pupils from each sample indicated that they disliked working on their own. Clearly, if teachers are able to take these preferences into account when planning lessons, they will be enjoyed by more pupils.

The fact that approximately 30 per cent of top primary pupils and 20 per cent of first-year secondary pupils indicated that for most, or all, lessons they counted the minutes till breaktime/the end of the lesson may be an expression of a lack of interest in the lessons, which may be alleviated to some extent by teachers including in their lessons the types of activities pupils enjoy (as described above). However, it is possible that the larger number of top primary pupils who find lessons too long could be explained by the fact that it is common practice for primary work to be approached using an integrated day, where pupils may work for extended periods of time on one or more areas of the curriculum. This is in contrast to the secondary schools' approach of dividing the school day into lesson periods of about 30 minutes, with some 'double' lessons of about one hour. It is therefore likely that first-year secondary pupils will change from one lesson to another more frequently than top primary pupils. In view of the responses from the primary age pupils, it may be worth primary schools adopting (at least in the top year) a more clear-cut timetable so as to give pupils a clearer end to particular lessons.

The fact that about three-quarters of pupils spend considerable periods of time each day either watching television or videos, or playing computer games (77 per cent of top primary and 81 per cent of first-year secondary spent two hours or more watching television and about 75 per cent of both groups spent some time each day playing computer games), means that pupils will be used to viewing colourful material with, in some cases, special video effects. It is not clear whether or not pupils would welcome increased use of audio-visual aids as part of lessons. However, it is undoubtedly true that pupils enjoy these media, as evidenced by the substantial number spending significant periods of time viewing them each day.

Our survey found that about half of the pupils in each age group indicated that they had never talked to their class teachers about their work during the school year. Fewer than one in ten of each sample reported that they had often had such talks. Since this would seem to be an ideal opportunity for teachers to provide feedback to their pupils and help to encourage and motivate their future efforts, it is unfortunate that few pupils appeared to have this opportunity: it would seem to be one area where schools could try to improve their practice.

6.3.2 Outside the classroom

Schools could also note that many of the positive comments made by pupils were concerned with the general friendly atmosphere of the school and the caring, supportive approach of the teachers. The smaller number of negative comments tended to focus on particular aspects of school life (such as dirty toilets and no opportunity to take pop or bottled water to school as part of a packed lunch) and the characteristics of a small number of teachers (such as sarcasm and alleged sexism).

Our findings with regard to bullying may give cause for concern. The apparent prevalence reported by both primary and secondary pupils has already been noted. Whilst details of individual pupils' interpretations of what comprises bullying were not available in this study, the fact that about ten per cent of the top primary and 15 per cent of the first-year secondary pupils chose to make comments about bullying indicates that for some pupils it is a significant part of their school life (although it should be noted in this context that some of the comments were favourable ones, i.e. 'There is no bullying in my school'). However, it is likely that teachers could increase their efforts to monitor and reduce the incidence of bullying within schools. Much useful information, together with constructive suggestions, is included in Tattum and Herbert (1990).

6.4 Further research

This study was cross-sectional. It compared the attitudes of two different groups of pupils, one of which was a year older than the other. It suggested that pupils' attitudes towards school and learning become slightly less positive as they mature. It is not possible to tell from a cross-sectional study whether individual pupils who disliked school and school work whilst at primary school also dislike their secondary schools. It could be that different children change their opinions in different directions so that some of those who expressed negative opinions about their primary schools in 1994 will express positive opinions about their secondary schools in 1995 and vice versa. This question is the focus of a subsequent longitudinal study in which we followed up the top primary school pupils taking part in this study by asking them to complete the questionnaire again after approximately one year in secondary school. We hope to report the findings in 1996.

REFERENCES

HALSEY, A.H. (Ed) (1972). *Educational Priority. Volume 1: EPA Problems and Policies.* London: HMSO.

KEYS, W. and FERNANDES, C. (1993). *What DO Students Think About School?* Slough: NFER.

KINDER, K., HARLAND, J., WILKIN, A. and WAKEFIELD, A. (1995). *Three To Remember: Strategies For Disaffected Pupils.* Slough: NFER.

LAPOINTE, A.E., MEAD, N.A. and ASKEW, J.M. (1992). *Learning Mathematics.* Princeton, N J: Educational Testing Service, Centre for the Assessment of Educational Progress.

ROBINSON, W.P. (1990). 'Academic achievement and self-esteem in secondary school: muddles, myths and reality', *Educational Research and Perspectives,* **17**, 1, 3-21.

TATTUM, D. and HERBERT, G. (1990). *Bullying: a Positive Response. Advice for Parents, Governors and Staff in School.* Cardiff: Cardiff Institute of Higher Education.

WEDGE, P. and PROSSER, H. (1973). *Born to Fail?* London: Arrow Books.

BACKGROUND INFORMATION ON THE SCHOOLS AND PUPILS

A1.1   School catchment and intake information

A total of 79 schools (38 primary and 41 secondary) took part in the study.

The sample of 38 primary schools included 20 schools with an age range of 5 - 11, six schools with an age range of 7 - 11 and nine schools with some other age range; three primary schools did not provide this information. Year 6 was the top year in all the primary schools taking part in the study.

The sample of 41 secondary schools consisted of 23 11-18 schools, 13 11 - 16 schools and two 11 - 14 schools; three secondary schools did not provide this information.

The schools taking part in the study were asked to provide information on their catchment area. Their responses are shown in Table A1.1.

Table A1.1   Type of catchment area: comparisons between the primary and secondary schools.

	Primary		Secondary	
Total	38	100%	41	100%
Mainly country town and/or rural....................	14	37%	20	48%
Mainly suburban	9	24%	13	32%
Mainly urban/inner city	12	31%	4	10%
Missing response...	3	8%	4	10%

Nearly 40 per cent of the primary schools described their catchment areas as 'mainly country town and/or rural, almost a quarter selected 'mainly suburban' and nearly a third opted for 'mainly urban/inner city. Compared with the primary school sample, the sample of secondary schools contained proportionally more schools with 'mainly country town and/or rural' catchment areas (nearly half), slightly more schools with 'mainly suburban' catchment areas (nearly a third) but proportionally fewer 'urban/inner city' schools (ten per cent). These differences between the two samples of schools, although at face value quite large, were not statistically significant at the five per cent level.

The schools also provided information on the proportion of pupils receiving free school meals. Details of the proportions of ethnic minority pupils and pupils with reading ages more than two years behind chronological age were also sought but, because of the high level of non-response to these questions, these data are not included in Table A1.2.

Table A1.2   Percentage of pupils receiving free school meals: comparisons between the primary and secondary school samples

Sample	Mean	s.d.	N
Primary	21.8	23.9	32
Secondary	13.6	11.0	34

Missing information: 7 schools

The sizes of the primary and secondary schools taking part in the study are shown in Tables A1.3 and A1.4.

Table A1.3   School size: primary schools

No. on roll	No. of schools	% of schools
100 or less	7	18
101 - 200	8	21
201 - 300	7	18
301 - 400	7	18
401 - 500	6	16
Missing information	3	8
Total	38	100

Table A1.4   School size: secondary schools

No. on roll	No. of schools	% of schools
500 or less	2	5
501 - 750	8	20
751 - 1000	14	34
1001 - 1250	8	20
1250 - 1800	6	14
Missing information	3	7
Total	41	100

A1.2 Background information provided by the pupils

Pupils were asked to indicate whether they were male or female, and the number of brothers and sisters they had. Their responses are shown in Table A1.4.

Table A1.5   Personal details: the responses of top primary and first-year secondary pupils

	Primary		Secondary	
Total	1265	100%	1009	100%
Male	628	49.6%	495	49.1%
Female	635	50.2%	508	50.3%
Missing	2	0.2%	6	0.6%
Number of brothers and sisters				
Five or more	65	5.2%	49	4.8%
Four	76	6.0%	41	4.1%
Three	177	14.0%	124	12.3%
Two	337	26.6%	259	25.6%
One	536	42.3%	437	43.4%
None	68	5.4%	92	9.1%
Missing	6	0.5%	7	0.7%

The proportions of boys and girls were equal for each age group. Similarly, the percentages of pupils with different numbers of brothers and sisters were broadly the same at each age group. Approximately four out of ten pupils in each sample had one brother or sister (42 per cent of top primary and 43 per cent of first-year secondary) and about a quarter of pupils from each age group had two brothers and/or sisters.

Pupils were asked to indicate the approximate number of books (excluding magazines, newspapers and comics) in their home. This measure, which has been extensively used in international comparisons of achievement, provides an indication of the cultural background within pupils' homes. Pupils' responses are shown in Table A1.6.

Table A1.6   Number of books in the home: the responses of top primary and first-year secondary pupils

	Primary		Secondary	
Total	1265	100%	1009	100%
0-10	57	4.5%	42	4.2%
11-25	156	12.3%	103	10.2%
26-100	341	26.9%	275	27.2%
101-250	300	23.7%	232	23.0%
251-500	194	15.3%	189	18.8%
More than 500	206	16.3%	154	15.3%
Missing	11	0.9%	14	1.4%

The information provided by pupils suggested that there were no differences in the cultural background for two age groups. Roughly half of each sample had a total of 26-250 books in their home, with the remaining pupils at each group having either more or fewer books.

ADMINISTRATION AND RESPONSE RATES

It was intended to achieve samples of about 1250 top primary (Year 6) and 1000 first-year secondary (Year 7) pupils. A total of 85 schools was selected for the top primary sample and 80 schools for the first-year secondary sample; this represented approximately twice the number of schools required to achieve the totals of 1250 and 1000 pupils from Year 6 and Year 7 respectively. Previous experience had shown that roughly a 50 per cent response rate could be expected, hence twice the number of schools required were originally contacted.

Timetable	
Schools invited to participate	9th May 1994
Questionnaires dispatched to schools	6th June 1994
First reminder (written)	13th July 1994
Second reminder (telephoned)	18th July 1994

Table A2.1   Response from schools

	Primary	Secondary
Schools drawn in sample and invited to participate	85	80
Agreed to participate	47	50
Refused	3	10
No reply	35	20
Sent questionnaires*	41	44
Returned completed questionnaires	38	41
Response rate from schools initially contacted	55%	63%
Response rate from schools sent questionnaires	93%	93%

*   *Six schools from each sample agreed to take part, but were not sent questionnaires as they had all already been allocated to other schools.*

The reasons given by schools for refusal to take part are listed below:

	Primary	Secondary
Unable to help	1	5
No time/pressure of work	2	4
Too many requests for surveys	-	1
Total	3	10

Table A2.2   Number of questionnaires dispatched and returned

Pupil questionnaire	Primary	Secondary
Questionnaires dispatched	1494	1183
Completed questionnaires received	1264	1009
School questionnaire		
Questionnaires dispatched	41	44
Completed questionnaires received	36	39

Completed pupil and school background questionnaires were not received from three schools from each sample for reasons including: lost in post, staff circumstances prevented administration, original questionnaires not received by school.